ARCHAEOLOGY
AND THE
DEAD SEA SCROLLS

VAUX, Roland de. Archaeology and the Dead Sea scrolls; the Schweich lectures of the British Academy, 1959. Oxford, 1973. 142p il map. 12.00. ISBN 0-19-725931-6

CHOICE   OCT. 73
Religion

Father de Vaux was the director of the archaeological excavations at the Dead Sea scroll community, caves, and farm center, and a member of the international team of scholars formed to prepare the manuscripts for publication. He was well qualified to present the archaeological evidence and its meaning for the study of the scrolls. Two years after he delivered the Schweich Lectures for the British Academy they were published in French; the work was immediately recognized as a major contribution. Before his death in 1971 Father de Vaux revised the manuscript and supervised its translation into English. His original conclusions remain unchanged, but several paragraphs are added to Chapter 1, a three-page appendix to Chapter 2, and numerous paragraphs and pages to Chapter 3. The book contains 38 plates, three line-drawings, one pottery chart, and an index. There is no other comparable book. The translation is well done. Highly recommended to scholars, university and college students, and interested laymen.

ARCHAEOLOGY AND THE DEAD SEA SCROLLS

BY

R. DE VAUX

O.P.

THE SCHWEICH LECTURES
OF THE BRITISH ACADEMY
1959

LONDON
PUBLISHED FOR THE BRITISH ACADEMY
BY THE OXFORD UNIVERSITY PRESS
1973

Oxford University Press, Ely House, London W. 1

GLASGOW NEW YORK TORONTO MELBOURNE WELLINGTON
CAPE TOWN IBADAN NAIROBI DAR ES SALAAM LUSAKA ADDIS ABABA
DELHI BOMBAY CALCUTTA MADRAS KARACHI LAHORE DACCA
KUALA LUMPUR SINGAPORE HONG KONG TOKYO

ISBN 0 19 725931 6

*Published in French in 1961; reissued with
revisions in an English translation in 1972*

*Printed in Great Britain
at the University Press, Oxford
by Vivian Ridler
Printer to the University*

FOREWORD

F R. ROLAND DE VAUX, whose Schweich Lectures delivered in December 1959 before the British Academy are here published, albeit somewhat altered and expanded, requires no introduction. His distinguished record of work in Palestinian archaeology, whether in the field or in the study, is well known to a wide circle of readers in England and elsewhere, and any attempt to appraise his achievement can be but an impertinence. All that needs to be said, then, is that Fr. de Vaux as Director of the École Biblique et Archéologique in Jerusalem has been closely connected with the Judaean Scrolls found in the caves round Qumran from the first discovery in 1947 and that he has presented reports, which are models of accurate scholarship, of the progress of the work carried out by himself and his team of colleagues at regular intervals. Here he sums up what has been done up to date.

The importance of the task can hardly be overrated; for, however much scholars may differ on minute points of interpretation, the significance of this or that detail or the exact date to which the documents or each document ought to be attributed, all (or almost all) are agreed that the group of Scrolls as a whole must be assigned to the most momentous period of human history, approximately that between the second century B.C. and the first or perhaps the second century A.D., between the Maccabaean age and the formative years of the early Christian Church. What enhances their importance, great as it is for the Jewish history of the period, is that, although contemporary Greek and Latin documents abound, no written Jewish works (other than a few inscriptions on tombs, an odd papyrus, and so on) survive in their original Hebrew form between the Book of Daniel and the Mishnah; all that is extant of Jewish literature is in translation.

The quality of Fr. de Vaux's work is apparent on every page. The lectures stand out as containing a fair and accurate statement of the facts as well as a sober appreciation of the interpretation that may be put on them; and, if nothing sensationally new appears in them, the absence of such matter may be taken as a guarantee of objective truth, so that they may be recommended to all who are interested in the subject as a safe guide through, and a great enrichment of, knowledge in a new field of historical research.

G. R. DRIVER

Magdalen College
Oxford, 1961

FOREWORD TO THE REVISED ENGLISH EDITION

IT is sad that Roland de Vaux did not live to see the translation of his Schweich Lectures appear. Qumran and the Dead Sea Scrolls occupied his attention for many years. I hesitate to say that the subject was his favourite one, for he entered into so many scholarly studies with tremendous enthusiasm; nevertheless, it was very near his heart.

All who heard him give the Schweich Lectures in 1959 will have no doubt of this enthusiasm. He lectured in English with enormous verve and fluency, with occasional engaging mispronunciations at which he would laugh as well as anyone. They were the only Schweich Lectures that I can remember which were crowded at the first lecture and more crowded by the end.

This publication of his lectures is a monument to his skill as an excavator, as a historian, and as an authority on the Scrolls themselves. It is a completely authoritative statement of the archaeological evidence, and this to an archaeologist seems conclusive for the dating of the Scrolls.

His death has deprived Palestinian archaeology and Biblical studies of a man of ripe wisdom and very great charm.

KATHLEEN M. KENYON

Oxford, 1972

PREFACE

AT the beginning of the summer of 1947[1] the first 'Dead Sea Scrolls' were accidentally discovered by some Bedouin shepherds in a cave situated near the north-western shores of the Dead Sea. This cave was identified by an officer of the Arab Legion and subsequently excavated by an expedition jointly undertaken by the Department of Antiquities of Jordan, the Palestine Archaeological Museum, and the École Archéologique Française de Jérusalem at the beginning of 1949.[2] At the time, although a surface survey in the site of the Khirbet Qumran ruins had been undertaken, it had not seemed to have any evident connection with the discoveries in the cave. However, at the end of 1951 representatives of the same institutions returned there and the soundings which they made brought to light pottery which was identical with that which had been discovered in the first cave, and also coins which established its approximate date.[3] Thereupon it was decided to undertake a complete excavation of the ruins, and this was continued in four further

[1] According to a statement attributed to one of the Bedouin, Muhammed edh-Dhib, the actual date of the discovery was 1945, W. H. Brownlee, *Journal of Near Eastern Studies*, XVI, 1957, pp. 236–9. This assertion was made in reply to questions put in 1956, and it cannot be allowed to invalidate the information supplied far earlier and spontaneously by the Bedouin and his companions, cf. Discoveries in the Judaean Desert, I, *Qumran Cave I*, 1955, p. 5; *Revue biblique*, LXVI, 1959, p. 88, n. 3. These doubts have been shared by J. C. Trever, 'When was Qumran Cave I Discovered?', *Revue de Qumran*, III. 1, February 1961, pp. 135–41. In his reply W. H. Brownlee makes certain concessions: 'Edh-Dheeb's Story of his Scroll Discovery', *ibid.*, III. 4, October 1962, pp. 483–94; 'Some New Facts Concerning the Discoveries of I Q', *ibid.*, IV. 3, October 1963, pp. 417–20. After a long inquiry J. C. Trever proposes as the date of the first discovery Nov.–Dec. 1946 or possibly Jan.–Feb. 1947, *The Untold Story of Qumran*, 1965, pp. 103 f., 169 f., 174. The Syrian Archbishop, Athanasius Yeshue Samuel has given his version of the story, *Treasure of Qumran. My Story of the Dead Sea Scrolls*, 1966, pp. 141 ff.; it was during Holy Week of 1947, cf. p. 137, that he heard the manuscript spoken of for the first time. I would now be inclined to correct the phrase 'at the beginning of the summer of 1947' to 'at the beginning of the year 1947'.

[2] *Revue biblique*, LVI, 1949, pp. 234–7; 586–609; D. Barthélemy and J. T. Milik, Discoveries in the Judaean Desert, I, *Qumran Cave I*, 1955.

[3] *Revue biblique*, LX, 1953, pp. 83–106.

campaigns from 1953 to 1956.[1] In the last of these campaigns
the search was extended to 'Ain Feshkha, three kilometres to the
south, where a building was located which had been completely
buried. This, together with its annexes, was laid bare in 1958.[2]
In the meantime the discovery of a second cave with manuscripts
by the Bedouin in 1952 had led to a systematic exploration of
the rocky cliffs above Qumran by the Palestine Archaeological
Museum, the American School of Oriental Research at Jerusalem, and the École Archéologique Française.[3] Shortly afterwards, but still in 1952, the Bedouin opened up a new cave, this
time in the marl terrace, and this prompted the archaeologists
to return to Qumran. They emptied this cave of its contents and
found another cave nearby, likewise containing fragments of
manuscript.[4] Finally, at the beginning of 1956, the Bedouin
penetrated into a cave in the cliffs, the entrance of which had
become blocked, and took several important manuscripts from it.
This cave was cleared of its contents by the archaeologists in the
course of the final season of excavations at Khirbet Qumran.[5]

All these discoveries have aroused enormous interest, and it is
justifiable that interest in them should be concentrated above all
on the texts which have in this way been made available to us.
But the archaeologist can make a contribution to the understanding of the texts by indicating the nature of the setting in
which they were discovered and so perhaps making it possible to
reconstruct the character of the human group from which they
emerged. It is for this reason that when the British Academy did
me the honour of inviting me to give the Schweich Lectures in
December 1959 I chose as my title 'Archaeology and the Dead
Sea Scrolls'. In the three lectures I gave I dealt only with the
archaeological aspects of the discoveries. I sought to avoid drawing any premature conclusions, and so to set forth as objectively
as possible first the results of the excavations at Khirbet Qumran
(the first lecture) and then those of the researches undertaken in
the Qumran region as far as 'Ain Feshkha (the second lecture).

[1] *Revue biblique*, LXI, 1954, pp. 206–36; LXIII, 1956, pp. 533–77.
[2] *Ibid.*, LXVI, 1959, pp. 225–55.
[3] *Ibid.*, LX, 1953, pp. 540–61; M. Baillet, J. T. Milik, R. de Vaux, O.P.,
Discoveries in the Judaean Desert, III, *Les 'Petites Grottes' de Qumrân*, pp. 3–17.
[4] Cf. *Revue biblique*, LX, 1953, p. 86; Discoveries . . ., III, p. 26.
[5] Cf. *Revue biblique*, LXIII, 1956, pp. 573–4.

It was only after this (in the third lecture) that a connection was established between the manuscripts discovered in the caves and the ruins which were excavated in the area. An attempt was also made to arrive at an historical explanation of the archaeological findings and to establish the extent to which they can throw light upon the interpretation of the texts. In these lectures only the discoveries made in the Qumran region were taken into consideration. Those made in the caves of Murabba'at and in other caves situated further to the south in the desert of Judaea, as also the discoveries at Khirbet Mird to the west of Qumran, have deliberately been omitted both from the lectures and the present volume. Their significance is different from that of the discoveries at Qumran. Those of Murabba'at and the southern area are essentially connected with the Second Jewish Revolt, while those at Khirbet Mird relate to the Christian and Arab epochs. Everything is to be gained by according a separate treatment to these other 'Dead Sea Scrolls' and so avoiding the confusions which are sometimes introduced.

In this volume the text of the original lectures has been reproduced with only slight development of their original form. Advantage has however been taken of certain observations which have been made to me, as well as of some more recent studies, notably some new identifications of the coins of Qumran and Feshkha made by Fr. A. Spijkerman, O.F.M., who is preparing the definitive catalogue of them. Some notes have been added in order to provide the relevant references to the archaeological material and the literary sources which have been used. It was the wish of the British Academy that fairly plentiful illustrations should be provided to take the place of the lantern-slides that were used at the actual lectures. The book makes no pretence to be anything more than a synthesis, or to provide more than a general orientation arising from the preliminary reports which have appeared in the *Revue biblique* between 1949 and 1959. Meanwhile we await the definitive report on the excavations at Qumran and Feshkha, which it is planned to publish in the series entitled Discoveries in the Judaean Desert.

R. V.

Jerusalem, Easter, 1960

PREFACE TO THE REVISED
ENGLISH EDITION

THE Schweich Lectures of 1959 on *Archaeology and the Dead Sea Scrolls* were initially delivered in English, but the British Academy then graciously agreed to publish the French text which I had prepared. Now it has requested an English edition. It was impossible simply to produce a translation of the original volume, now more than ten years old. It is true that during this time the author has not undertaken any further exploration in the Qumran region, and that he does not find it necessary to modify in any essential point the conclusions which he then put forward. But he has had to take into account certain studies which have been published since that time, as well as some more recent excavations and new theories which have resulted in a different interpretation being placed on the archaeological evidence. The effects of this revision are discernible throughout the volume, but it has particularly affected Chapter III, in which the element of interpretation is most strongly to the fore.

The author wishes to express his thanks to the British Academy for having initiated the publication of this volume, and also to his friend David Bourke for having so competently discharged his task as translator.

R. V.

Jerusalem, June, 1971

CONTENTS

LIST OF PLATES

The plans in Pls. III, IV, VI, XVII, XXIII, XXXIX, XLI were drawn up by Fr. H.-M. Coüasnon. The map in pl. XL was designed by Mr. Jack Ziegler. The table of illustrations in pl. XLII was drawn by M. Antoine Hazou. The photographs were provided by the following: Pl. I: Fr. A. Strobel, O.M.I.; Pl. IX: Abbé J. Starcky; Pls. II, v*b*, VII*b*, VIII*b*, X*a*, XII, XIV, XV, XVI, XVIII, XIX*a*, XX*b*, XXI, XXII, XXIV*b*, XXVIII, XXIX, XXXII*b*, XXXIII, XXXIV, XXXV*b*: The Palestine Archaeological Museum. Pls. v*a*, VII*a*, VIII*a*, X*b*, XI, XIII, XIX*b*, XX*a*, XXIV*a*, XXV, XXVI, XXVII, XXX, XXXI, XXXII*a*, XXXV*a* and *c*, XXXVI, XXXVII, XXXVIII: École Archéologique Française de Jérusalem.

I

KHIRBET QUMRAN

KHIRBET QUMRAN is the name of a site with ruins
which lies a little more than one kilometre to the west of
the shores of the Dead Sea. It is situated on a low plateau
of marl which runs parallel to the seashore at this point, between
the rock cliffs and the littoral plain. Khirbet Qumran occupies
an outcrop of this marl plateau. To the south it is bounded by
the steep declivity of the Wadi Qumran, to the north and west
by ravines. Only a narrow neck of the marl joins the outcrop to
the main part of the plateau (Pl. I). Towards the east the ground
slopes away quite steeply, and here traces have been discovered
of an ancient path leading up to the settlement. Prior to the
excavations the only remains actually recognized as such were
some piles of stones and a cistern which had become almost
completely filled in. Eastwards from the ruins, and extending
over the sloping ground, lies a vast cemetery, but previously the
connection between this and the buildings had not been established. Now, as a result of some five campaigns of excavation,
a complex of buildings has been uncovered which extends eighty
metres from east to west and about a hundred metres from north
to south (Pl. II). On the basis of an examination of the walls and
the various soil levels, and of a study of the pottery and coins,
it has been possible to distinguish several different periods of
occupation and to assign dates to them.

I. ISRAELITE REMAINS

The first human settlement at Khirbet Qumran goes back to the
Israelite period.[1] The foundations of some of the walls are on a
lower level than others, being embedded in a layer of ash containing numerous sherds of Iron Age II. Among the areas in which
these sherds have been found the following are particularly

---

[1] *Revue biblique,* LXIII (1956), 535–7.

noteworthy: the angle between loc. 73 and loc. 80,[1] extending beneath loc. 68, the outside of loc. 6 and loc. 40, to the north of loc. 38 (throughout this area they are associated with the remains of earlier walls), and against the foundations of the eastern wall of loc. 38. They are again to be found *against* the north wall of loc. 77, the foundations of which are very deep, and *beneath* the south wall of the same locus, which has much shallower foundations and has been superimposed on a thin layer of ash containing Israelite sherds only. This same layer reappears beneath locs. 86 and 88. Among the sherds found beneath loc. 68 we should notice in particular a jar-handle stamped with the inscription 'to the king', *lammelek*, belonging to a series well known from other contexts, and an ostracon inscribed with some letters in palaeo-Hebrew characters.

The location of the sherds and the levels of the foundations of the walls provide evidence to help reconstruct a coherent plan. It is of a rectangular building comprising the following features: a large courtyard; a row of rooms running along its eastern wall with one projecting outwards at the north-east corner; other less clearly identifiable features against the north and south walls (Pl. III). This plan approximates to the plans of the Israelite strongholds which have been explored in the Plain of the Buqei'a, on the plateau which dominates Qumran,[2] as well as in the Negeb, at 'Ain Qedeirat and elsewhere.[3] The wall running along the eastern edge of the cistern at 117 represents the containing wall of the building to the west, but in front of this and on the same side there is an enclosure defined by the walls of locs. 106, 109, 113, 114, 119 *bis*, and 108. This enclosure had an opening to the north between locs. 114 and 119 *bis*, through which the draining of the surface water was guided into a large round cistern, 110 (Pl. v*a*). This is the deepest of the cisterns at Khirbet Qumran as well as being the only one that is round. Although, as a result of having been re-utilized in the subsequent period and so cleaned out at regular intervals, it did not contain

---

[1] The position of the *loci* is shown on the schematic plan in Pl. xxxix.

[2] F. M. Cross and J. T. Milik, 'Explorations in the Judaean Buqê'ah', *Bulletin of the American Schools of Oriental Research*, **142** (Apr. 1956), 5–17.

[3] In particular Khirbet Ghazza, cf. Y. Aharoni, 'The Negeb of Judah', *Israel Exploration Journal*, VIII (1958), 33–5.

any Israelite sherds, it is nevertheless almost certain that it goes back to this time. As I have said, we have been able to establish affinities between this building at Qumran and certain other fortified buildings. And whenever these were not situated near a spring, as is the case with that at Qedeirat, they included at least one cistern. A final element which can be assigned to this first period of settlement is a long wall running from the southeast corner of the ruins and extending right to the Wadi Qumran, thereby serving to demarcate an esplanade to the south of the buildings.[1] This has exactly the same orientation as the eastern wall of the Israelite building, and the manner in which it is built, with large blocks, closely resembles the construction of the surviving part of the north wall. Furthermore, this wall certainly seems to be earlier than the constructions of the subsequent periods, to which it has been linked by a slanting extension exhibiting a different type of masonry.

The date of this settlement can be established from the sherds. Nothing here is earlier than the eighth century B.C., and the latest date which can be assigned to the settlement as a whole is the end of the seventh century. This date is confirmed by the stamped inscription *lammelek*, belonging to the final period of the monarchy, as well as by the ostracon, for the lettering on this belongs to a period not very much earlier than the Exile. Everything points to the fact that this settlement did not survive the downfall of the kingdom of Judah, and the ashes which are consistently associated with the Israelite sherds indicate that it suffered a violent destruction.[2]

II. PERIOD I*a*

Khirbet Qumran had been in ruins for a very long period when a fresh human group came to settle there. The two occupations are separated from one another by an interval of several centuries, so that no connection can be established between them. Thus a fresh phase began in the history of the site, and the excavations have enabled us to reconstruct its various stages.

---

[1] It begins in loc. 78 to the east of the cistern 71; it is partly visible on Pls. II and III.

[2] The historical identification of this establishment will be discussed in chap. III, pp. 71-3.

This is Period I*a* (Pl. iv),[1] and its beginnings were modest. What remained of the Israelite buildings served as a point of departure for the constructions of the new occupants. A channel was built to collect the water which drained on to the esplanade to the north of the ruins and to provide more effective means of supplying water to the round cistern. At the side of this two other cisterns, 117 and 118, this time rectangular ones, were dug out, and a decantation basin where the silt was deposited, common to the three cisterns, was constructed (Pl. v*a*). In addition to this a small channel was built leading to one of the new cisterns, and it passed under the Israelite wall so as to collect the water flowing in from the south. Here too the corner which had been left open in the earlier plan was closed in and provided with one or two covered buildings, locs. 101–2.

To the north of the containing wall by which the round cistern had formerly been enclosed, some rooms were added, locs. 115–16 and 125–7. Still further to the north of this complex several minor rooms are to be found, locs. 129, 133, 140, 141, which are assigned to Period I*a*, since in the following period the walls of these were cut through in order to allow for the building of a drain, and at the same time some of them fell into disuse.

In the area to the east the plan of Period I*a* is less clear. It is certain that the eastern and southern lines of the Israelite building were retained. The northern line, where the destruction had been greater, may have been reconstructed at this period and henceforward have acquired a slightly different outline. Precisely what constructions were put up inside this enclosure at this time it is not easy to say. Possibly the new settlers contented themselves with repairing some of the rooms on the eastern side. Those to the south-east were not rebuilt, and on the site where they had once stood two potter's kilns were built side by side (Pl. v*b*). In the following period one of these was destroyed while the other was partly obliterated when some steps were built leading down to a cistern, loc. 66.[2] There is nothing to indicate that these kilns were already in service during the Israelite

[1] *Revue biblique*, LXIII (1956), 537–8.

[2] A very similar kiln dating from the Hellenistic epoch has been discovered at Pella (Macedonia), *Bulletin de correspondance hellénique*, LXXXIX (1965), 800, fig. 7.

period. Certain traces of the new phase of occupation are to be found elsewhere, but these do not constitute elements from which a consistent plan can be reconstructed.

It is difficult to determine with any precision the time at which this installation took place. Only some sherds and a few pieces of pottery found beneath the later levels in the southern area of the main building can be attributed to it. This pottery is indistinguishable from that of Period I*b*, and there are no coins associated with it. For this reason the chronology can be established only approximately by its relation to the better documented period which follows. As we shall see, the coins indicate that the buildings of Period I*b* were certainly occupied under Alexander Jannaeus, 103–76 B.C., and that they may have been constructed under John Hyrcanus, 135–104 B.C. This construction marks the concluding date of Period I*a*. It is possible that this would have commenced under one of the predecessors of John Hyrcanus, but we cannot push it back very far because the modest nature of the buildings and the scarcity of archaeological material attest the fact that this first installation was of short duration. Very soon an impressive complex of buildings was raised on the plateau of Qumran, obliterating the ancient Israelite fort. Its outermost lines were preserved, but lost their significance, and as a result of this new complex of buildings the establishment of Period I*a* was greatly enlarged.

III. PERIOD I*b*

This period, when the buildings at Khirbet Qumran acquired what was virtually their definitive form, we have called Period I*b* (Pl. VI).[1] The main entrance was at the centre of the north front at the foot of a solidly built tower, locs. 9–11. Leading up to this was a track, the outline of which can still be discerned. Coming from the north it led across the plain extending from the shores of the Dead Sea and so up on to the plateau.

---

[1] *Revue biblique*, LXI (1954), 208–10, 214–16; LXIII (1956), 538–45, 551–77. (By an error the store of pottery in loc. 114, p. 562 and fig. 4, has been attributed to Period II because it includes three 'Herodian' lamps. But these lamps are rougher in design than true 'Herodian' lamps and are earlier than these. The group as a whole belongs to Period I*b*. Moreover, the locus was covered by Period II.)

Another and smaller gateway was set on the north-western side, loc. 139, from which it was possible either to proceed along the foot of the cliffs or to ascend to the plain of the Buqei'a and so to Jerusalem by a path which was ancient and perhaps already in existence in the Israelite period. This path climbs up the rocky formation by a series of hairpin bends just to the north of Wadi Qumran.[1] There was also a third entrance, probably on the eastern side, near a potter's kiln at loc. 84.

On entering the main gateway to the north one would have found on one's right a large courtyard, where the remains of buildings belonging to Period I*a* still survive. The buildings lay to the left of this entrance: viz. a main building to the east and a lesser building to the west, separated by an open space containing the group of three cisterns belonging to Period I*a* and the rooms of the same period, now re-utilized as workshops. There was only one means of access to this complex of constructions: a gateway which has almost entirely disappeared between the two buildings at loc. 128.

On the north-west corner of the main building stood a massive two-storey tower, locs. 9–11.[2] The various rooms of the lower storey opened into each other but there was no door leading to the outside, and apart from two narrow apertures in the north wall they were devoid of windows. They could only have served as store-rooms and the way into them would have been down a spiral staircase (of wood?), the supporting column of which has been preserved in the south-east corner, loc. 8. On the upper storey there were, apart from this staircase leading downwards, three rooms with an external doorway opening on the south face. But the only way of reaching this doorway on the first floor was by a wooden balcony extending over two small courts, locs. 12 and 13, and leading to a terrace on the south-west of the whole complex. The fact that the builders were especially preoccupied with considerations of defence is brought out still more clearly by the isolated position of this tower, for it was separated from the

---

[1] Cf. M. Baillet, J. T. Milik, R. de Vaux, *Les 'Petites Grottes' de Qumrân*, Discoveries in the Judaean Desert, III (1962), 6 and Pl. II 1; S. Schulz, *Zeitschrift des Deutschen Palästina-Vereins*, LXXVI (1960), 58–9 and Pl. 7 A.

[2] The plan in Pl. VI shows the arrangement of the elements on the ground floor for Period I*b*. The plan in Pl. XVII shows how the elements on the upper storey were arranged, and this remains the same for Periods I*b* and II.

rest of the buildings by the open spaces in locs. 12 and 18. To the south at the foot of the tower a gateway and a passage at locs. 12 and 17 gave access to the installations on the east. A neighbouring gateway led into a little court, loc. 13, and this in turn gave access to the rooms on the south-west. One of these rooms, in which a bench runs along the walls, loc. 4, has the appearance of being an assembly room. The long room next to it in loc. 30 could have had a similar function. From the little courtyard a staircase led up to the terrace at loc. 4 and to the floor which lay above rooms 1, 2, and 30.

To the east of this complex was a courtyard, bounded on the north by a rectangular room with a paved floor, locs. 38 and 41, the function of which at this period is uncertain. Probably it was already being used as a kitchen as it was in the following period, when several fireplaces were installed there. From this one could pass into a narrow courtyard to the north,[1] as well as into the rooms on the east, locs. 39, 40. In the southern part of the large courtyard there are some buildings of which the arrangement and purpose remain uncertain, in particular several small basins, the water from which was emptied by a system of channels extending towards the east, loc. 34. Further to the east of the courtyard and separated from it by a wall there was an open space without covering where two cisterns had been dug, 49, 50. Steps led down into the larger of these, loc. 48, and they had been superimposed on the pottery kilns of the earlier period. At the side was a washing-place with a stone basin and a large sump, loc. 52, followed by a store-room where a quantity of iron tools was found, loc. 53.

The installations last mentioned backed on to the eastern wall of the old Israelite building. From this a new wall led away obliquely to join the long wall bounding the esplanade to the south. In the triangular space thus formed the small store-rooms or workshops were demarcated from one another by partitions of brick, locs. 44, 45, 59–61. In this area too a potter's workshop had been set up, a feature to which we shall return.

[1] The existence of this courtyard and its containing wall to the north is conjectural, this part of the plan having been altered during the following period. But it is unlikely that in this complex of buildings which has been so carefully enclosed there would have been three doors near to one another, those of locs. 18, 40, and 41, giving directly on to the outside of the buildings.

To the south of the main building a large stepped cistern had been dug, locs. 56, 58. On the other side of this a long room had been built on the outside of the Israelite wall, loc. 77. At a later stage we shall be discussing the function of this room and the annexe attached to it.

During Period I*b* a less important building was added on the western side. It comprised a courtyard, loc. 111, and two long elements, locs. 120 and 121, divided by partitions. The compartments thus formed were evidently used as store-rooms. The space between the two buildings was already taken up by the three cisterns and the rooms of Period I*a*. The use to which these were put at the period with which we are here concerned has not been determined. Probably, as in the subsequent period, they served as covered workshops. To the south of this entire complex there was yet another large deep cistern, loc. 91, and a courtyard bounded by a wall overhanging the ravine to the west, loc. 96. Against this wall a less strongly constructed 'lean-to' had been built, of which only a few elements have survived, loc. 97. This has tentatively been interpreted as a stable for the pack animals. Further to the south and extending to the Wadi Qumran stretched a bare esplanade bounded to the west by the ravine and to the east by the containing wall of the Israelite period.

The most striking feature of this plan is the number and the importance of the cisterns. The extension of the buildings and the increase in the number of the settlers in Period I*b* made it necessary, in effect, to provide for a more plentiful and more constant supply of water. It was at this time that an aqueduct was built to catch the water brought down by the winter rains into Wadi Qumran. At some points it was hewn out of the rock while at others it was dug into the marl terrace, and it served to conduct the water into the settlement.[1] At this point it changed into a channel carefully coated with an impermeable plaster identical with that found in the cisterns, and at least for some part of its course it was covered with stone slabs. This channel wound its way between the buildings and served to feed the various cisterns (Pl. vII*a*). In front of each cistern or group of cisterns was placed a decantation basin to keep the water clean.

---

[1] Description and schematic plan of the aqueduct in S. Schulz, *Zeitschrift des Deutschen Palästina-Vereins*, LXXVI (1960), 53–8.

The cisterns were uncovered, and in summer the contents would have evaporated very quickly. In the winter, on the other hand, though Wadi Qumran filled with water only on isolated occasions, when it did so the quantity far exceeded the capacity of the cisterns. All this meant that there had to be a basin at the point where the aqueduct started so as to regulate the flow of water. Since it is impossible to discern any trace of masonry this must have been a natural basin, namely the circle of rocks which can still be seen, although its eastern edge has been partly carried away by natural accidents.

Proceeding from the wadi the aqueduct culminated in a sluice-gate at the north-west corner of the Khirbeh, where the flow was interrupted by piles of masonry, loc. 137. The water spread out in a wide shallow decantation basin, locs. 132, 137. Near this basin a bath was built, loc. 138 (Pl. viiia). This was reached from the north by an open doorway near the point where the aqueduct entered, and probably from the east also by a gangway linking it to the main courtyard, 135. The water thus purified flowed out of the basin by a channel leading out of its south-eastern corner and was conducted into the buildings through a breach in the wall of Period Ia. It first filled the round cistern 110 and the two neighbouring cisterns 117, 118, which were already in existence during the preceding period. Since this channel was at a higher level than that of Period Ia the walls of the round cistern were heightened, a new decantation basin was installed, loc. 119 *bis*, and other subordinate channels served to regulate the flow of water to the three cisterns. The overflow from the cisterns and the water used in the various industries in this area was carried off by means of a drain which can be traced northwards to the point where it leads to the outside of the settlement.

From this point onwards the channel turned towards the south-east and opened out into a small decantation basin, 83. From this the water flowed out on the west side into a large rectangular cistern, 85, 91, and on the east into the continuation of the channel. From this point the channel went on to fill the long cistern, 56, 58, to the south of the main building, and then wound round its northern side, crossing a small square basin at 67 and turning back again in a southerly direction. At this corner a side channel led off to feed the two cisterns on the eastern side, 49, 50. From this point the channel led on through a breach in the Israelite wall to supply a small bath, 68 (Pl. viii*b*), and after that a final decantation basin, 69, before culminating in a large cistern at 71 situated to the south-east of the ruins (Pl. vii*b*). The overflow of water from the system as a whole was conducted from the two large cisterns on the south-west and south-east by means of gutters which gradually petered out on the esplanade.

This highly developed and carefully constructed water system is the most striking characteristic of Khirbet Qumran. It reflects the needs of a group which was relatively numerous, which had chosen to live in the desert, and for which, accordingly, the problem of how to ensure a supply of water was vital. At a later stage we shall have to raise the question of whether this explanation is sufficient, and whether the multiplicity of cisterns does not suggest something more than this, namely that the settlers were obliged by rule to observe certain purification rites.[1]

But this water system is only one element in a plan which is remarkable chiefly for its qualities of unification and organization. Khirbet Qumran is not a village or a group of houses; it is the establishment of a community. We must be still more precise: this establishment was not designed as a community residence but rather for the carrying on of certain communal activities. The number of rooms which could have served as dwellings is restricted as compared with the sites designed for group activities to be pursued. The buildings added on to the west comprise simply a courtyard and some store-rooms. The lower storey of the tower is also taken up by store-rooms. If the correctness of our interpretations is accepted, there is only a single large kitchen, a single large washing-place, and one stable. There are several workshops and several assembly rooms.

One of these latter, that at loc. 4, near to a small courtyard in the south-western quarter of the main building, had had a low bench installed round its walls from Period I*b* onwards. In one of its walls two recessed cupboards had been inserted. In another wall near to the door a small basin had been carved out which could be filled from the outside. This feature gives the appearance of having been designed for closed sessions in which those

[1] Cf. p. 98.

taking part did not wish to be disturbed, and thus as a kind of council chamber. Beside it was a larger room, loc. 30, which at this period was equipped with a broad entrance bay. This could have been used for assemblies involving larger numbers.

The most important feature of all is to be found to the south of the main building (Pl. IXa) at loc. 77. This is a room 22 m. long and 4·50 m. broad, and orientated east and west. It has two doors, one near the north-western corner, the other near the south-eastern one, and opening on to the large esplanade. This is the largest room in the whole of the ruins, and it is clear that it was a meeting-place. Towards its western extremity a circular area stands out from the surrounding plastered floor by the fact that it is paved. This seems to mark the place where the president of the assembly would have taken his stand.

But this large room was not used only as a meeting-place. In Period Ib its floor slopes gently from the western extremity to the door giving on to the southern part of the esplanade. Then the floor rises slightly as far as the containing wall to the east. Furthermore, a conduit leading out of the main channel has its opening in this room near the north-western door. This conduit could easily be opened or closed. The fact that water was brought into the room in this way, combined with the sloping of its floor, made it easy for the room to be washed, the water being carried off to the outside by way of the south-eastern door. This arrangement indicates that it was necessary to clean the room at frequent intervals and suggests that it also served as the refectory.

Close at hand one finds evidence to confirm this hypothesis. Near the president's place a door opens on to an adjoining room which extends to the south of the main room and is at right angles to it, loc. 86, 89 (Pl. IXb). This room suffered an unusual degree of damage in an earthquake, which put an end to Period Ib, and of which we shall have to speak again later on. The ceiling fell in and under the debris of this we found a stock of more than a thousand vessels.[1] They had been stacked at the

---

[1] The attribution of this group of pottery to Period Ib has been disputed by J. T. Milik, *Dix ans de découvertes dans le Désert de Juda* (1957), 44. In *Revue biblique*, LXVI (1957), 635, I have given the archaeological reasons which in my opinion make it necessary to uphold the date which I here maintain to be correct. J. T. Milik has discussed these arguments in the English

end of the room. To the west were heaped 21 small jars of two different types, 38 dishes, and 11 jugs. Against the pilaster 210 plates had been piled (Pl. x*b*). In the eastern part 708 bowls were arranged in piles of a dozen each so as to form a rectangle (Pl. x*a*). In front of these lay 75 beakers. Some other pieces of pottery of the same type were scattered over the floor. This was not the community's store-room for pottery in general since many of the forms in current use, frequently found elsewhere in the ruins, are missing here, such as the large jars, the lids, the pots, the juglets, the lamps, etc. It was not in any ordinary sense an annexe to the potter's workshop since that is situated in another area. This store must have a connection with a use to which the main room adjoining it was put. As it happens these vessels comprise everything that would be needed for meals (Pl. xv*a*): jars to distribute the water, jugs and beakers from which to drink, dishes from which to serve the food, plates and bowls for eating. This, then, was the crockery, stored near the assembly-room, because that room must also have been used as a dining-room.

Some, at least, of these meals seem to have had a religious significance. In the free spaces between the buildings or round them the excavations have laid bare animal bones deposited between large sherds of pitchers or pots (Pl. x1*b*), or sometimes placed in jars left intact with their lids on. In one instance such bones have been found covered simply by a plate. In the

---

edition of his book, *Ten Years of Discovery in the Wilderness of Judaea* (1959), 55. However, with regard to the wall of Period II, which in my opinion divided the room into two and shut off the part containing the pile of broken crockery, he has failed to recognize that this is not the thin line of stones to which he refers, but rather a solid wall which was built at that time on either side of the central pillar. This wall cannot possibly belong to Period III. On the other hand the crockery (especially the plates and beakers) clearly belongs to the pottery group of Period I*b* and is different from that of Period II which has been found on the upper level of the large room. Now let us turn to the argument from palaeography. The name אלעזר had been scratched on one of the bowls before it was baked and, so Milik argues, the lettering is typical of the writing of the first century A.D. I am doubtful whether five letters (scratched, and not traced with a pen as are the manuscripts to which he compares these letters) can overthrow the sum total of the archaeological indications. The ascription to Period I*b* is confirmed by P. Lapp, *Palestinian Ceramic Chronology, 200 B.C.–A.D. 70* (1961), 50–1.

majority of these cases the sherds come from several jars or pots to which fragments from one or more bowls, lids, or plates have been added. As a rule these deposits have hardly been covered with earth. They are flush with the level of the ground. Some of them even seem to have been laid on the ground. To the north of the secondary building in loc. 130 two pots containing bones were uncovered by the flood which overflowed from the large decantation basin after the earthquake. They were carried along in this flood and were covered by the sediment which it left behind.

The places in which such deposits were discovered are very varied. Briefly, they appear with varying frequency in almost all the open spaces of the Khirbeh.[1] The most numerous group, comprising some thirty examples, took up a large part of loc. 130 between the secondary building and the large decantation basin (Pl. xia). Some thirteen of these deposits were discovered in the course of digging a trench two metres in width along the wall bounding the southern side of the large esplanade, and it seems certain that if the whole of this space were cleared many others would be found.

The date of these deposits is determined by the level at which they were discovered, the pottery covering them, and in some instances by the coins which were recovered from their immediate vicinity. The majority belong to Period I*b*. This applies to those taken from the trench to the south and to most of those buried to the north of the secondary building, loc. 130. These latter were, moreover, covered by the sediment which accumulated during the time when the site was abandoned between Periods I*b* and II. The pottery is characteristic of Period I*b* and some coins of Alexander Jannaeus have been discovered nearby. But the same custom persisted during the following period. Such deposits have been discovered above the sediment of loc. 130 and in the old decantation basin, loc. 132, which was no longer in use. They are covered by sherds belonging to Period II and associated with coins of Agrippa I and the Procurators.

The bones from thirty-nine of these deposits have been examined by Professor F. E. Zeuner of the London Institute of

[1] They are marked by small circles on Pl. vi for Period I*b* in locs. 23, 80, 92, 130, 135, and on Pl. xvii for Period II in locs. 73, 80, 130, 132.

Archaeology. No single deposit contains the complete skeleton of any animal. The bones had been taken apart, and the flesh was no longer attached to them when they were collected up. Twenty-six of these deposits contain bones coming from a single animal, nine of them the bones from two animals, three the bones from three animals, and one the bones from four different animals. The species represented are as follows, with a small margin of uncertainty with regard to the number of animals involved: adult sheep 5, adult goats 5, bones belonging indistinguishably either to sheep or goats 26, lambs or kids 10, calves 6, cows or oxen 4, and one unidentified animal of the height of a small cow.[1]

These bones are certainly the remnants of meals. Most of the bones are clean but some have been charred, which shows that the meat was generally boiled and sometimes roasted. They represent only one part of the refuse accumulated in the refectory or the kitchen. The general purpose underlying this custom is plain. The care with which the bones were set apart after the flesh had been cooked and eaten reveals a religious preoccupation. It is possible that these are the remnants of sacrifices in which the victim, or some part of it, was eaten by the faithful,[2] though this has not been proved. For sacrifice of any kind an altar is necessary and the excavations have not brought to light any altar or any place adapted to the ritual sacrifice of victims. On the other hand, these deposits do constitute clear evidence of the fact that certain of the meals eaten in the main chamber which we have described had a religious significance.[3]

[1] Cf. F. E. Zeuner, 'Notes on Qumrân', *Palestine Exploration Quarterly* (1960), 27–36.

[2] This is the opinion of F. M. Cross, *The Ancient Library of Qumran and Modern Biblical Studies*, 2nd edn. (1961), 69–70 and 101–2 (all references in this volume will be to this second edition of the English original. In 1967 a German version appeared entitled *Die antike Bibliothek von Qumran und die moderne biblische Wissenschaft*. This version was partially revised and expanded, and a supplement was added, mainly to bring the bibliography up to date as far as 1966). However, a point that we must notice with regard to the deposits of bones is that nothing corresponding to this ritual is to be found in the sacrificial regulations of the Jews. What remained from the communion sacrifices had to be burned, Lev. 7: 17, and this also applied to the remains of the Passover victim, Ex. 12: 10. Nothing is said about the bones.

[3] J. Kaplan has excavated a cemetery near Tel Aviv which ranges in date between the first and fourth centuries B.C. Here, near to the tombs, a trench

Another aspect of the communal life at Qumran is illustrated
by the presence of several workshops. Those set up between the

has been discovered containing the bones of oxen and sheep mingled with
fragments of pottery, 'The Excavation of an Ancient Cemetery Near Tel
Baruch', *Bulletin of the Israel Exploration Society*, XVIII (1954), 163–7. He has
likewise discovered animal burials dating from the fourth century B.C. in an
ancient Jewish cemetery of Tell Qasileh near Jaffa. He puts forward the
hypothesis that the firstborn of clean animals would have been buried in this
way. This custom has survived in certain Jewish communities of Europe and
North Africa, and he relates it to the deposits of bones at Qumran, *ibid.*, XXII
(1958), 97 and *Revue biblique*, LXV (1958), 412–13. He has suggested to me in
a private letter that the people of Qumran were seeking to remain faithful to
the law of Deut. 15: 19–20 by eating the firstborn as communion sacrifices.
Being unable to fulfil this ritual at Jerusalem as was prescribed, they would
have preserved the bones. It may be objected that, in contrast to these other
discoveries, all the deposits at Qumran are outside the cemetery. Against the
hypothesis that they would have been the remains of sacrifices of firstborn
animals, the reservations which we are about to make with regard to sacrifices
at Qumran in general apply here too.

J. van der Ploeg, *Journal of Semitic Studies*, II (1957), 172–3, puts forward
the hypothesis that the Qumran community regarded the bones of animals
as impure, and that their purpose in burying them in pots or beneath sherds
was to avoid anyone touching them inadvertently while digging in the earth.
This hypothesis seems very far-fetched.

K. Schubert, *Die Gemeinde vom Toten Meer* (1958), 27, 50, considers that the
bones were carefully buried for the reason that at the time of the religious
repast blessings were pronounced over the meat, and that bones thus conse-
crated could not simply be thrown away without regard. This solution is
reasonable and may be retained in default of any text giving the true
explanation of this rite.

Finally E. M. Laperrousaz, *Numen*, VII (1960), 60–8, suggests that the pots
and bones were not deliberately buried, but rather abandoned on the spot
when a festal banquet was tragically interrupted by an enemy attack. This
would have taken place on two occasions, a little before 63 B.C. and in A.D. 68.
There are no real grounds to support this hypothesis. Nevertheless the author
of it has again come to its defence in *Revue de l'Histoire des religions*, CLX
(1961-B), 1–9, and in *Semitica*, XII (1962), 98–104.

H. Bartdke, 'Die Tierknochenfunde auf Chirbet Qumran', *Lehre, Forschung,
Praxis. Die Karl-Marx-Universität Leipzig zum zehnten Jahrestag ihrer Namens-
gebung am 5. Mai 1963*, 328–49, seeks to explain the custom in terms of two
factors suggested by ethnology: the belief that the animals involved would
return to life, and the maintenance of the unity of the community which the
covenant meal was intended to achieve.

S. H. Steckoll, 'The Qumran Sect in Relation to the Temple of Leontopolis', *Revue de Qumran*, VI, 1 (Feb. 1967), 55–69; 'Marginal Notes on the
Qumran Excavations', *ibid.*, VII, 1 (Dec. 1969), esp. p. 36, compares these
deposits to the animal bones discovered by Flinders Petrie at Tell el-
Yahudiyeh-Leontopolis in domestic ovens. In both cases, he suggests, these

two buildings have been preserved only in the form they acquired in Period II, and it is in this form that they will be described. But we know of three workshops belonging to Period I*b*: the small basins set in the southern part of the courtyard of the main building, loc. 34, the precise function of which has not been determined, the washing-place against the eastern wall of the same building, loc. 52, and finally the potter's workshop (Pl. XII).

This workshop was set up in the south-eastern area in place of the ovens of Period I*a* and is in an exceptionally complete state of preservation.[1] The potter washed his clay in a shallow and carefully plastered basin, loc. 75 (Pl. XIIIa). The water which he needed was brought by a conduit leading off the main channel which flowed into a little cistern next to the basin. It may be asked whence this craftsman obtained his clay. The marl of the terrace of Qumran can be made into excellent mud bricks but it is too calcareous and not malleable enough to be used as potter's clay. Nor are there any beds of clay in the immediate environment of Khirbet Qumran. We might wonder whether the potter could have made use of the deposits which formed in the cisterns and decantation basins. There is clay on the plateau above the Dead Sea and the winter rains carried it down into Wadi Qumran. From there the aqueduct carried it to the Khirbeh where it was deposited in the cisterns. But the analyses undertaken by Professor F. E. Zeuner have shown that these deposits, which could make excellent mud bricks, were still far too calcareous for a potter's work.[2] We do not know, therefore, from what source the potter would have obtained his clay. I can only point out that the engineers of the new Arab Potash Company have discovered an excellent layer of clay to the north of the Dead Sea. This is not too far from Khirbet Qumran.

However that may be, the potter did have clay, and when he had cleaned it he stored it in a pit where it was left to mature, loc. 70. The final mix was made in a shallow tank adjoining this

would constitute the remains of sacrifices for the consecration of a sanctuary. I would still adhere to the reply to this which I have given in *Revue biblique*, LXXV (1968), 204–5.

[1] *Revue biblique*, LXIII (1956), 543–4; LXVI (1959), 97.

[2] F. E. Zeuner, 'Notes on Qumrân', *Palestine Exploration Quarterly* (1960), 27–36.

pit. Opposite it was the site of the wheel in loc. 65 (Pl. xiiib). It was a circular cavity made of stones, and the potter, sitting on the edge, used his feet to maintain the motion of the wheel, the flat top of which was on a level with his hands. The potters of Hebron still have, to this day, exactly the same way of doing their work. The kilns were close at hand. There were two of these. The first, loc. 64 (Pl. xiva), was designed for the larger pieces. These were put into the oven through an opening in the upper part and arranged on a bench. The fire was laid through an opening in the lower part, to which several steps led down, loc. 84. In this same locus, and opposite the first kiln, there was a second for the smaller pieces (Pl. xivb). It consisted of two chambers one above the other separated by a shelf pierced by flues. This is a very ancient type, and examples of it have been found in Palestine, at Tell el-Far'ah in the north, which go back to as early as the beginning of the third millennium B.C.[1] The draught of the large kiln was from the north, while that of the small one was from the south. These directions correspond to the prevailing winds in the Dead Sea depression, and the potter could always use one or other of his two kilns.

This workshop was the source of most of the large number of vessels discovered at Khirbet Qumran, and the fact of local manufacture explains both the monotony of the pottery and at the same time its unique character as compared with other sites of the same epoch (Pl. xlii). It also explains why particular traditions should have been preserved there, as well as the fact that the pottery of the two periods Ib and II is very similar. Many of the forms are common to both periods, yet there are certain differences. One type of jar is confined to Period Ib. It is ovoid in shape with the neck strengthened from the outside (Pl. xvb, right). There is only one exact counterpart to it and this was found in the excavations of the Citadel of Jerusalem at a level belonging to the third century B.C. and long before the reign of

---

[1] Cf. *Revue biblique*, LXII (1955), 558–62. For instances which, although outside Palestine, are closer in date to these examples compare the kilns of Tell el-Farâ'în in Egypt, which belong to the Ptolemaic epoch and the beginning of the Roman epoch, D. Charlesworth, *Journal of Egyptian Archaeology*, LIII (1967), 150–2; LV (1969), 23–6, and the kiln at Volubilis in Morocco from the second century A.D.; C. Domergue, *Bulletin d'archéologie marocaine*, IV (1960), 491–505.

Herod.[1] The plates belonging to Period I*b* are simple in outline
(Pl. xv*a*) and never have the moulded edge exhibited by some
of the plates of Period II. The distinguishing marks of the
beakers are still clearer. Those of Period I*b* are large, flared, and
have a very fine wall (Pl. xv*a*). Those of Period II are smaller,
thick, and generally ribbed. The distinction is clearest in the
case of the lamps, and is particularly valuable in their case as a
distinguishing characteristic because the different types are
known, and their dates firmly established, from other excavations. The lamps of Period I*b* are to be assigned to the end of the
Hellenistic period, those of Period II belong to the beginning of
the Roman period. In this latter series there are many lamps of
the type known as 'Herodian', while others may be assigned to
types already known to belong to the first century A.D.

From the comparisons which can be drawn between the
pottery of Khirbet Qumran and that of other sites it can be
established that Period I*b* belongs approximately to the end of
the Hellenistic epoch. The coins enable us to achieve a still
greater precision. They have been found in considerable numbers
but are much oxidized, and it is only after prolonged treatment and close study that it has been possible to identify some
four-fifths of the whole collection.[2] Those of Period I*b* begin with
eleven coins of the Seleucids. There are six silver coins, of which
three are dated precisely as falling within the reign of Antiochus
VII in 132/131, 131/130, 130/129 B.C. Three others do not bear
any legible date but two of them can be attributed to Antiochus
VII (one uncertain) and the third to Demetrius II (uncertain). It
must be remembered that the silver coins remained in circulation over a long period, and are of little use for dating an
archaeological level apart from providing a vague *terminus post*

[1] C. N. Johns, 'The Citadel, Jerusalem', *Quarterly of the Department of
Antiquities in Palestine*, XIV (1950), 144 and fig. 14.

[2] The lists given in *Revue biblique*, LXI (1954), 230 and LXIII (1956), 565,
were provisional, not all the coins having been cleaned and identified. In the
course of preparing the definitive list Fr. A. Spijkerman, O.F.M., has made
notable additions to these lists and has changed a certain number of the
ascriptions either as a result of better readings or by reference to the most
recent studies which have appeared on Hasmonean coins. At this point I
quote the actual results of his work. The few identifications which still
remain to be made will not seriously affect the general picture which can
now be presented.

quem. But there are five small Seleucid bronzes from the reigns of Antiochus III, Antiochus IV, and Antiochus VII without any precise date.[1] It must be remarked at this point that it was not until the reign of John Hyrcanus I (135–104 B.C.) that the Seleucid currency was replaced in Palestine by a Jewish currency, that John Hyrcanus himself only began to strike his own coins at a fairly late stage in his reign,[2] and that even then the Seleucid coins continued in circulation. On the other hand the finds of Khirbet Qumran include only a single coin which can certainly be assigned to the reign of John Hyrcanus I.[3] It may be remarked that coins from his reign rarely appear in sales of antiquities. The finds include one coin of Judas Aristobulus (104–103 B.C.) but 143 coins of Alexander Jannaeus (103–76 B.C.), the Hasmonaean for whom by far the largest number of coins were struck. For the following period there is one coin of Salome Alexandra and Hyrcanus II (76–67 B.C.), five coins of Hyrcanus II (67 and 63–40 B.C.), four coins of Antigonus Mattathias (40–37 B.C.). The coins of Herod the Great I shall reserve for later discussion.

The interpretation of the coin evidence is a delicate matter. It is certain that the buildings of Period I*b* were occupied under Alexander Jannaeus. It is possible that they were already built under John Hyrcanus. Arguments might be drawn from the Seleucid coins, which continued to circulate during his reign, but these coins could have survived from Period I*a* even though we have not been able to assign any of them definitively to that phase.[4] In any case the fact that there are so few Seleucid bronzes makes it very difficult to regard Period I*b* as beginning before John Hyrcanus.

[1] To this must be added a small bronze of Antiochus IV found by a visitor, R. R. Williams, 'An Early Coin from Qumran', *New Testament Studies*, VIII (1961–2), 334–5.

[2] After the conquest of Samaria in 110 B.C. according to B. Kanael, 'The Beginning of Maccabaean Coinage', *Israel Exploration Journal*, I (1950–1), 170–5; according to L. Kadman, 'The Development of Jewish Coinage' in *The Dating and Meaning of Ancient Jewish Coins and Symbols* (Numismatic Studies and Researches, II. Publications of the Israel Numismatic Society) (1958), 88, this would have been after the death of Antiochus VII and the disintegration of the Seleucid empire in 129 B.C.

[3] Correcting the premature identifications in *Revue biblique*, LXI (1954), 230; LXIII (1956), 565.   [4] Cf. p. 5.

With regard to the end of Period I*b* we have two pieces of evidence: an earthquake and a fire. The effects of the earthquake are particularly apparent in the two cisterns situated in the eastern area of the main building. The steps and the floor of the largest of these cisterns, locs. 48, 49 (Pl. xvi) have been split and the whole of the eastern part has sunk to about 50 cm. lower than the western part. There was a vertical cleavage which left the walls standing, although the north wall of the cistern was split from top to bottom and its eastern portion sank following the movement of the earth. The crack was prolonged into the neighbouring cistern, loc. 50, the floor of which was clearly torn away, and the track of it can be traced right across the ruins of this period to the north and south of the two cisterns. Other parts of the buildings were equally affected. The tower was shaken; its eastern wall was cracked. The lintel and ceiling of the lower chamber fell in. The north-west corner of the secondary building was likewise damaged, and was in danger of collapsing into the ravine immediately below it. In the southern region the signs are less clear, except in the annexe of the large room, the back of which fell in, burying the pottery store of which we have spoken.[1]

Certain indications supplied by Flavius Josephus[2] enable us to fix the exact date of this earthquake. In the seventh year of Herod the Great, just as preparations were being made for the Battle of Actium between Caesar and Antony, a terrible earthquake ravaged Judaea, killing 30,000 men and many animals. At the time Herod was making war against the Nabataeans. His army, which had encamped in the Plain of Jericho, did not

[1] Cf. *Revue biblique*, LXI (1954), 210 and 231–2; LXIII (1956), 544. In two articles, 'The Qumran Sect in Relation to the Temple of Leontopolis', *Revue de Qumran*, VI, 1 (Feb. 1967), esp. 69, and 'Marginal Notes on the Qumran Excavations', *ibid.*, VII, 1 (Dec. 1969), esp. 33–4, S. H. Steckoll attributes the following opinion to T. Zavislock, the expert attached to the English Historical Monuments Service, who directed the measures of conservation at Khirbet Qumran: that there was neither an earthquake nor any cessation in the occupation at Qumran. The faults in the cisterns at 48, 49, 50 would have been caused 'by the weight of water introduced upon the first use after the building or repair of these cisterns'. I do not know whether this represents an accurate account of the opinion of T. Zavislock. In any case this explanation cannot be accepted.

[2] *Ant.* xv. v. 121–47; *Bell.* I. xix. 370–80.

suffer any losses but was thrown into a state of great terror. The Arabs of Transjordan, receiving exaggerated reports of the catastrophe, believed that the Jews were at their mercy and massacred the ambassadors who had arrived with proposals for peace. Herod gathered his soldiers and restored their courage. This cataclysm, he told them, was merely an accident of nature and it had passed. Alternatively, if it was considered to be a divine chastisement it should be recognized that God had brought it to an end and that by sparing the army he had given a pledge of victory. Then, having offered a sacrifice, Herod crossed the Jordan and proceeded to pitch his camp opposite Philadelphia-Amman. The earthquake which so terrified the soldiers stationed in the Plain of Jericho is the same as that which damaged the tower and cisterns of Khirbet Qumran, and its date has been recorded by the Jewish historian: the spring of the year of the Battle of Actium, the seventh year of Herod's reign, that is the spring of 31 B.C.[1]

The end of Period I*b* is likewise marked by a fire in the buildings. In the covered areas, which were cleaned out at the time when they were reoccupied, few traces of this can be discerned. Nevertheless there are some. The embrasure of the communicating door between the two elements in the south-east corner of the main building, locs. 1 and 4, had been burned at some point earlier than that at which it was blocked up in Period II. But the most important piece of evidence is a layer of ashes, thick in some places and thin in others, which extends over the open spaces in the vicinity of the buildings. The roofs of reed had been burned and the ashes had been spread by the wind.

The question may be asked whether the earthquake and the fire were simultaneous. My first thought on this point was that the earthquake had affected a building which had already been destroyed by fire and abandoned.[2] Later I gave up this solution,[3]

---

[1] On this date cf. W. Otto, 'Herodes' in Pauly–Wissowa, *Real-Encyclopädie* ... *Suppl.* II (1913), 46. E. Schürer, *Geschichte des jüdischen Volkes*, I (1920), 383. A. Schalit, *König Herodes, Der Mann und sein Werk* (1969), 122–3, n. 98, raises the question of whether the earthquake at Qumran could not have been that of 64 B.C. known to the Talmud and Dion Cassius. The presence of coins from the reign of Antigonus seems to me to exclude this.

[2] *Revue biblique*, LXI (1954), 235.

[3] *Ibid.*, LXIII (1956), 544.

but it has been taken up by other authors.[1] Their judgement is that the two events must be kept distinct. Khirbet Qumran, they think, was burned by the Parthians in 40–39 B.C. or by their ally the Hasmonaean Antigonus, who reigned from 40 to 37 B.C. The buildings would then have been ruined and empty at the time of the earthquake some years later. It is difficult to make any assured judgement. The presence of four coins of Antigonus—and coins from his reign are rare—is an indication at least that the fire and the abandonment must have taken place after the beginning of his reign, when the Parthians had left. In that case one might attribute the cause of this destruction to the insurrections which were resisted by Herod and Antigonus, certain episodes of which are to be located at Masada and Jericho.[2] Against this, however, the movements of the two opposing parties do not seem to have affected the actual area of Qumran itself.

On the other hand if Khirbet Qumran was still actively functioning in 31 B.C., and if, as a result of this, fires were still being lit there, it would not be surprising if the earthquake had unleashed a fire. None of the archaeological evidence runs counter to this solution.

At the same time, however, it is equally true that there is no evidence to confirm it. The coins in particular are not of much assistance here.[3] Actually ten coins of Herod the Great have been

---

[1] E. M. Laperrousaz, 'Remarques sur les circonstances qui ont entouré la destruction des bâtiments de Qumrân à la fin de la Période I*b* de leur occupation', *Vetus Testamentum*, VII (1957), 337–49; and 'Note additionnelle', *ibid.*, VIII (1958), 92–4; J. T. Milik, *Dix ans de découvertes dans le Désert de Juda*, (1957), 108–9, more cautiously in the English edition, *Ten Years of Discovery in the Wilderness of Judaea*, (1959), 52. In a more recent article in *Numen*, VII (1960), 26–76, E. M. Laperrousaz suggests that the date of the abandonment should be as early as between 67 and 63 B.C. He considers that it continued until the reign of the Procurators, or rather that the site would have been reoccupied during the reign of Herod the Great and abandoned for a second time on the occasion of the census of Quirinius in the sixth year of our era. It is not possible to discuss these hypotheses, which distort the evidence of stratigraphy, ceramics, and numismatics in the use they make of them. The author has put forward a further defence of his positions in *Semitica*, XII (1962), 75–86.

[2] Josephus, *Ant.* XIV. xv. 394–412; 448–50.

[3] Here I am correcting an earlier statement in *Revue biblique*, LXIII (1956), 566. On the coins from Trench A, cf. below p. 35.

identified, but we cannot use them to prove that the buildings of Period I*b* were still occupied at the beginning of his reign for two reasons. First, the place where they were found: they came from mixed levels, where they were associated with later coins. In the instance most favourable to the theory a coin of Herod was found together with four coins of Alexander Jannaeus, and one of Antigonus associated with a group of eight coins of Alexander Jannaeus but also close to a coin of the Procurators. The second point is their date. The coins belonging to Herod's reign, apart from the issues of the third year, which are not represented at Khirbet Qumran,[1] are not dated. An attempt has been made in a recent study to establish the chronology of the different coin types,[2] and according to this those that were discovered at Khirbet Qumran would have been in circulation only after 30 B.C. This dating is no more than probable, but if it is accepted then it follows that these coins of Herod do not belong to Period I*b*.

The question remains open, therefore, and my real reason for believing that the fire may have coincided with the earthquake of 31 B.C. is that this solution is the simplest and that there is no positive argument to contradict it.

However this may be, the buildings damaged by the fire or the earthquake were not repaired immediately. Once the water system had been dislocated it was not put into order again or maintained, and the water which still continued to come down from Wadi Qumran overflowed the Khirbeh. The sediment from this accumulated in the large decantation basin 132, overflowed it, and spread into loc. 130 as far as the wall of the building. This deposit lies above the layer of ash from the fire, and near the north-west corner of the secondary building it reaches a thickness of 75 cm. As it extends towards the east it

---

[1] However a coin from the third year has been found at 'Ain Feshkha in conditions which allow us to attribute it to the corresponding level in Period I*b* of Khirbet Qumran. Cf. below, pp. 65–6. This provides an indirect confirmation of the fact that the occupation of Khirbet Qumran would have continued until after the victory of Herod over Antigonus.

[2] J. Meyshan, 'The Coins of the Herodian Dynasty', *The Dating and Meaning of Ancient Jewish Coins and Symbols*, Numismatic Studies and Researches II. Publications of the Israel Numismatic Society (1958), 32. Y. Meshorer, *Jewish Coins of the Second Temple Period* (1967), 67–8.

grows progressively thinner. It is this sediment that provided the
foundation for a supporting wall which was put up to strengthen
the north-west corner during Period II. In the same way the
additional supports which were put up at this time round the
annexe and the assembly room, loc. 89, were not based directly
on the level which was in use in Period I*b*.

All this implies a period of abandonment, for it is highly
improbable that, as has been suggested,[1] some of the settlers
would have continued to live at Khirbet Qumran camping in
the ruins. They would at least have put the water system in
working order, for it was this that made life there possible. There
are admittedly the ten coins of Herod, which, as we have seen, are
very probably later than the destruction. But they do not prove
that there would have been an uninterrupted habitation of the
site, for they could have been brought there at the time when it
was reoccupied.[2]

IV. PERIOD II

The period of abandonment was in fact of short duration, and
the community which came to re-settle Khirbet Qumran was
the same as that which had left it. The general plan remained,
in effect, the same, and the principal elements were put to use
once more for the purposes for which they had originally been
intended. The necessary clearance and repairs were made, but
only secondary modifications were introduced to the buildings.
This is Period II (Pl. xvii).[3]

[1] J. T. Milik, *Ten Years of Discovery in the Wilderness of Judaea* (1959), 53–4.

[2] The smallness of their number implies, rather, that the site was abandoned during the reign of Herod, cf. the statistics assembled by B. Kanael,
'Some Observations on the Chronology of Khirbet Qumran' (in Hebrew),
Eretz-Israel, v (1958), 167. They are not even enough to prove that the site
was reoccupied before the end of this reign, cf. p. 26. These conclusions with
regard to a period of abandonment at Qumran during the major part of the
reign of Herod the Great have been confirmed by the excavations at Masada.
This palace-fortress, built by Herod, has yielded a rich harvest of objects
characteristic of his reign, which is unrepresented at Qumran, while the
correspondences between the two sites can be clearly established for the
following epoch, that which is the counterpart of our Period ii, cf. Y. Yadin,
'Qumran and Masada', *Yediot*, xxx (1966), 117–27 (in Hebrew); cf. *Revue
biblique*, lxxiii (1966), 229.

[3] Cf. *Revue biblique*, lxi (1954), 210–13; lxiii (1956), 545–7.

Most of the rooms were cleared out, a circumstance which has deprived us of many pieces of evidence which would have been valuable for Period I*b*. Some of the debris was carried out to the north of the ruins and left on the slopes of a ravine where it has been brought back to light by one of our excavation trenches, Trench A. It is clear that it was deposited there on one particular occasion for it contains only the pottery of Period I*b* and the corresponding coins.[1] Other parts of the debris were simply thrown outside the walls. They formed the heap at the foot of the north wall of the secondary building (Pl. xi*a*) and against the western wall of the same building.

However, no attempt was made to clear certain rooms which were too much encumbered, or of which it was decided to make no further use. The north room on the lower floor of the tower, loc. 10, the ceiling of which had fallen in, was condemned, and the communicating door between this and the room on the south side was blocked up. In the annexe of the main assembly room, locs. 86, 89, the broken crockery was left in its place and a wall was built of the same height as the central pillar. In order to make it easier to build this wall it may have been found necessary to clear a space through the debris so as to provide it with a firm base. This may explain why a parapet of stones was made to hold back the debris in the rear part of the annexe.

The structures which had been most damaged were strengthened. The large tower was consolidated by a belt of stones completely surrounding it but higher on the sides facing north and west which are on the outside of the building. This entailed the destruction of one room which had been built against the west wall of the tower, and the blocking up of the two light slits in the north wall. Although the primary purpose of this must have been to strengthen the tower, which had been rendered unstable by the earthquake, the ramp of stones thus formed gave the appearance of a rampart and increased the defensive potential of the works. The north-west corner of the secondary building, which threatened to slide into the nearby ravine, was likewise strengthened with a buttress. An extra thickness was added on the outside to the rear walls of the annexe to the assembly room, and above the double wall thus formed a door was pierced

[1] Apart from one exception, cf. p. 36.

in the south wall giving access to a new room, loc. 89, the floor
of which was laid above the accumulation of the crockery and
debris from Period I*b*. The two rooms at the north-east corner of
the main building, locs. 6 and 47, were reinforced from the inside.

New constructions introduced to modify the plan of the buildings were of little importance. In the secondary building the courtyard at loc. 111 became a covered space, and the long room to
the north was divided into two, locs. 120 and 122–3. In the space
between the buildings, apart from the workshops, to which we
shall shortly come, two adjacent structures, locs. 105, 107, inter-
rupt the harmony of the original plan. Loc. 105 contained the
community's baking oven. In the main building the room on
the south-western side was divided into two, locs. 1 and 2. The
communicating door between loc. 1 and the small assembly-
room at loc. 4 was blocked up, and in this same room the bench
already running along three sides was completed so as to run
along the south wall as well. In the long room adjoining, loc. 30,
the bay on the north side was blocked up and a new room was
built in the central court, loc. 33. But the main addition was a
room, no doubt a store-room, consisting of three compartments,
loc. 46. This was added on at the north-east corner and attached
to the buttressing of the tower by means of a wall so as to form
a courtyard, loc. 27, with a doorway near the corner of the
tower, loc. 19.

As far as the south of the building is concerned, we have
already pointed out the modification to the annexe to the large
assembly-room, locs. 86, 89. This room itself, loc. 77, had been
damaged by the earthquake or the fire, and the roof at least had
to be reconstructed. Three pillars were built with their bases on
the floor level of Period I*b*, and a pilaster was constructed against
the eastern wall (Pl. ix*a*). There was an economic reason for this.
Large beams were scarce and expensive, and the addition of
these supports made it possible to use shorter ones. The door
which opened on to the southern esplanade was blocked up. It
was no longer possible to introduce a copious stream of water to
cleanse the room as in Period I*b*, and the sloping of the floor levels
lost its purpose. The new floor was flat apart from one step in the
eastern section. Since it was no longer necessary to conduct
water into the room, the conduit which had been used for this

purpose was blocked up. These modifications and those to the annexe do not imply that the function of the room had changed. The platform at the western end remained uncovered, and the reason for not continuing the series of pillars throughout the whole length of the room appears to have been in order that the majority of those assembled might be able to see the president when he took his stand on this platform. In the same way the room continued to be used as a refectory. Some of the crockery has been found on the floor, being especially plentiful in the south-western corner, and some stands for jars were found scattered here and there. As in the earlier period, the meals which were eaten here had a religious significance and the same rituals were observed: deposits of animal bones similar to those of Period I*b*,[1] but covered with sherds from Period II and associated with coins from the same period, have been brought to light either in the same areas as those of the earlier period or elsewhere, as for example in the large decantation basin, loc. 132, which had lost its former purpose.

In fact the water system had been slightly modified. The sediment accumulated in this large basin was left uncleared, and only a small basin was maintained, situated near the sluice-gate at the entrance, loc. 137. The water from it was drained by a channel built along the eastern wall of the original basin and joining the earlier channel at the south-east corner of this basin. The long cistern to the south of the main building was divided into two, locs. 56, 58. The two cisterns on the eastern side, which had been split by the earthquake, locs. 49, 50, were abandoned, and the conduit branching away from the main channel to feed them was blocked up.

Since Period II was the last significant period of occupation, more information as to how the buildings were equipped and used on it can be obtained than on the preceding period. The large room to the east of the tower, locs. 38, 41, which I have already designated as a kitchen, had previously contained five fireplaces. The small basins in the south of the courtyard, loc. 34, were abandoned and covered over, no doubt because the conduit which carried away the used water had been severed by the earthquake. But it seems that the washing-place situated further

[1] Cf. pp. 12–13.

to the east, loc. 52, continued to be used in some form. The water which was needed now had to be drawn from the channel nearby. The potter's workshop, which was described in our account of the preceding period,[1] remained in use, and it seems that the only modification now introduced to it was that the drainage channel near basin 75, where the clay was levigated was given a slightly different course.

The chief points to which attention must be drawn are the installations in the space between the two buildings (Pl. xviii). In loc. 125 there was a workshop comprising a furnace above which was a plastered area with a drainage conduit (Pl. xixb). The installation implies that the kind of work carried on there required a large fire as well as an abundant supply of water. I do not venture to define its purpose any more precisely than that. To the south of the round cistern, loc. 101 (Pl. xixa) was furnished at this time with a solidly built pavement. A large furnace was built of small bricks which were exposed to fierce fire, with a smaller oven by the side. Set up on the pavement was a wooden cylinder coated with plaster, the purpose of which was to preserve some substance kept pressed down by a stone disc. The workplace as a whole was covered in and a flight of steps gave access to a terrace or rather an upper storey through which the mouth of the furnace chimney projected. No object has been found giving any clue to the meaning of all this, and I do not know what craft was practised there.

It is easier to interpret the function of an installation just beside this one. In the open space along the edge of the channel, loc. 100, there was a mill (Pl. xxa). A circular platform with a trough carved into its surface was built on a pavement of large stones. This is the place where the mill-stones were set up and it was into this trough that the flour fell. We discovered the two basalt mill-stones intact (Pl. xxb) in a pit which had been dug to the south of the mill during Period III, loc. 104. The broken remnants of two other mill-stones were also found here. This quarter, therefore, was the place where the corn was ground. An installation of this kind would seem to indicate that the people of Qumran cultivated corn or barley, for it would have been easier to buy flour than grain which they would then have

[1] Cf. pp. 15–16.

had to grind themselves. Corn-growing of this kind is not possible on the shore of the Dead Sea, but it can be practised in the plain of the Buqei'a which overhangs Khirbet Qumran to the west, and up to which, as we have said, an ancient pathway led.

We have already spoken several times of the long room which extends southwards from the tower, loc. 30, and which, being at ground level, could have served as an assembly room. During Period II the north bay had been blocked up and the final two metres at the southern end of the floor had been covered by a thick mat, the burnt remains of which have been recovered. The room was filled with the debris from the upper floor, which had the same plan, and which had fallen in at the end of Period II. In this debris were found fragments of structures made of mud-brick covered with carefully smoothed plaster. These mysterious fragments were collected and taken to Jerusalem where they were painstakingly re-assembled. In this way it was found possible to reconstruct a table from them (Pl. xxia) a little more than 5 m. in length, 40 cm. in breadth, and only 50 cm. in height. There were also further fragments from two smaller tables. These tables had certainly fallen from the upper floor where the long table had been set up parallel to the eastern wall; they had been used there in association with a low bench fixed to this wall. This might have suggested the furniture of a dining-room except for the fact that we had already identified this in another part of the buildings which did not contain a table. In any case it would have been most surprising for the refectory to be situated on an upper storey.[1] Furthermore two inkwells

---

[1] This last argument is invalid. G. R. Driver has reminded me of the upper chamber where the Last Supper took place, Mark 14: 15; Luke 22: 12, and this was the current practice, as is indicated by the use of the word *coenaculum* to designate the upper storey of a house. But I maintain that these tables do not constitute the furniture of a dining-room, as G. R. Driver attempts to show, 'Myths of Qumran', *The Annual of Leeds University Oriental Society*, vi, (1966–8), (*Dead Sea Scrolls Studies, 1969*) (1969), 23–7. He cannot point to any other dining-table, *abacus* or *mensa* in antiquity resembling this long narrow table associated with a bench running along the wall. What is more, he has not recognized that the low platform with two hollowed-out compartments illustrated in Pl. xxib was something different from the tables, and that these latter could not be compared to the tables equipped with cavities, *cavernae*, of antiquity. On the analogous theories of J. L. Teicher and H. E. Del Medico, cf. p. 31, n. 4.

were found among the debris, one bronze and the other earthen-
ware, of a type known, from discoveries made in Egypt and
Italy, to belong to the Roman period. One of these inkwells still
contained some dried ink. Is it not reasonable to regard these
tables and inkwells as the furniture of a room where writing was
carried on, a *scriptorium* in the sense in which this term later came
to be applied to similar rooms in monasteries of the Middle
Ages?

Against this it has been objected that ancient representations
do not show scribes or copyists sitting at a table. They are seated
on the ground or on a bench, sometimes with their feet on a
footstool, and they are writing on their knees. A different
approach is taken by some who accept the designation of this
element as the *scriptorium* but then go on to infer that the scribes
sat on the 'table' and put their feet on the 'bench' so as to raise
their knees.[1] Now this table is made of mud-bricks and is only
18 cm. broad at the base, and it is extremely doubtful whether
it could have supported the weight which, on this showing,
would have been placed upon it. Moreover, the purpose of
narrowing the table towards the base in this way seems to have
been precisely so that the scribe, who would have taken up a
squatting rather than a sitting position on the low bench, could
cross his knees and rest them against it. On the other hand it is
certainly the received opinion that in antiquity, and right down
to the eighth–ninth centuries of our era, writing tables did not
exist.[2] But there are certain witnesses to them which are far
earlier than this: a sarcophagus of the fifth century showing a
man sitting at a table to write, a mosaic from North Africa of the
fourth to fifth centuries representing an individual writing on a
papyrus scroll(?) which rests on a table, and finally a relief of
the third to fourth centuries A.D. from Ostia. Here two scribes are
shown sitting at low tables and writing on wax tablets. Between

---

[1] B. M. Metzger, 'The Furniture of the Scriptorium at Qumran', *Revue de
Qumran*, I. 4 (1959), 509–15. The author considers that his explanation
constitutes merely 'the least unsatisfactory theory', p. 515.

[2] Cf. in particular A. Dain, *Les Manuscrits* (1949), 22–3; T. C. Skeat, 'The
Use of Dictation in Ancient Book-Production', *Proceedings of the British
Academy*, XLII (1956), 183–4; above all B. M. Metzger, 'When did Scribes
Begin to Use Writing Desks?', *Akten des XI. internationalen Byzantinisten-
Kongress 1958* (1960), 355–62.

them another individual is speaking from a little dais on which he is standing. In the background are some people gesticulating. These are either stenographers recording a discourse or clerks attached to a court or, perhaps, clerks at an auction sitting on either side of the auctioneer and recording the bids of the purchasers.[1] We must also take into account a rather obscure passage in the Mishnah.[2] This distinguishes three kinds of *basisiyôt* which can incur certain impurities: the *basis* which lies before a bed or before scribes, the *basis* of a side-table, the *basis* of a cupboard. The word is borrowed from the Greek and in general signifies a rest; elsewhere in the Mishnah and Talmud it signifies a base, the base of a column, the foot of a candlestick, etc. In the context with which we are concerned it signifies a piece of furniture or some part of such a piece on which something is placed or supported and which is capable of contracting some impurity from this fact. The *basis* which is in front of the scribes seems to be a desk or table. This may be a table on which they place their writing materials, or it could equally well be the table on which they actually write.[3]

A further feature which has been reconstructed is a low platform which will have rested against the north wall of the same room (Pl. xxi*b*). This too is made of plaster. It has a surrounding rim and is divided into two hollowed out compartments each with a shallow cup-shaped cavity. We put forward the hypothesis that this would have been used for subsidiary acts of purification entailed in the copying or handling of the sacred books, for according to the Mishnah these 'soil the hands'.[4]

[1] These ancient representations are mentioned by B. M. Metzger, *loc. cit.* We are still waiting for an adequate publication of the Relief of Ostia. Cf. provisionally G. Calza, 'Scavi a Ostia', *Le Arti*, I (1938–9), pl. 120; H. Fuhrmann, *Jahrbuch des archäologischen Instituts. Archäologischer Anzeiger*, LV (1940), 439 and fig. 18. Through the kindness of Professor E. G. Turner I have obtained a photograph.

[2] *Kelim*, XXIV. 7.

[3] This is the solution of S. Krauss, *Talmudische Archäologie*, III (1912), 158: 'ein Gestell, Pult, auf welchem der Schreiber schrieb'.

[4] Above all *Yadaïm*, III. 3–5, IV. 5–6, with G. Lisowsky's commentary, *Die Mishna . . .*, VI. 11, *Jadajim*, 1956. H. E. Del Medico, *Le Mythe des Esséniens* (1958), 313–16, suggests that the platform with cavities is a *mensa* for funeral offerings and that the long table is that pertaining to a *triclinium*, and concludes that the whole would have been used at celebrations of the Christian agape. Cf. the earlier remarks of J. L. Teicher in *Journal of Jewish Studies*, V

One learned librarian,[1] while accepting that the two small tables would have been used for writing, has put forward the explanation that the long table would have been used for spreading out the scrolls, or for oiling them so as to keep them supple as well as for repairing them. This is certainly possible, but we cannot exclude the fact that it may also have been used as a writing table. It has the same shape and the same dimensions (apart from its length) as the small tables. Once we admit the hypothesis that the room was a *scriptorium* we can look for the place where the books were stacked, and for this the librarian suggests loc. 4, which is situated in the same block but on the ground floor, and which we have interpreted as a council chamber. On the alternative hypothesis the bench running along the walls would have served to support the wooden racks in which the scrolls were stored. This does not seem very probable, for despite the fact that this bench and the plaster covering the walls are in a relatively good state of preservation they show no trace whatever of any shelves or racks of this kind having been fixed to them. Furthermore, the bench and the walls have been replastered on several occasions, which implies that they were not covered up. If books were kept in this room it is more probable that they would have been piled in the two niches in the south wall. In this same wall, but on the side nearest to loc. 2, there is another niche which could have served the same purpose, and between this niche and the north-eastern corner of the room a high bench was built which could have served better than that in loc. 4 as a support for shelving. These are only conjectures and these three niches could equally well have served as cupboards for general use. We do not know, therefore, where the bookstore was,[2] but our ignorance on this point makes

(1954), 147. In *Revue biblique*, LXVI (1959), 108–9, I have stated the reasons for holding that these hypotheses are impossible.

[1] Mrs. K. Greenleaf Pedley, 'The Library at Qumran', *Revue de Qumran*, II. i, no. 5 (Nov. 1959), 21–41.

[2] The parallels adduced by Mrs. Greenleaf Pedley from the great libraries of antiquity do not carry much conviction. In particular the stand running parallel to the walls in the libraries of Ephesus, Pergamum, etc. is very different from the bench of loc. 4 and does not have the function which she attributes to it. Cf. B. Götze, 'Antike Bibliotheken', *Jahrbuch des deutschen archäologischen Instituts*, LII (1937), 225–47; R. Triomphe, 'Sur le dispositif intérieur des bibliothèques antiques', *Revue archéologique*, 1938–II, 248–51

no difference to the interpretation which can be given of the room containing the table and the inkwells. The hypothesis that it was a *scriptorium* remains the most probable. It was on the upper storey and was constructed with brick walls (we found the debris of these on top of the fragments of the tables). No doubt too it was equipped with large bays opening towards the east and affording a good light.

The pottery of Period II is very plentiful (Pls. XXII and XLII). Certain forms have already been noticed for purposes of comparison with those of Period I*b*.[1] There are certain unique features which underline the autonomy of Khirbet Qumran, where, as we have said, there was a manufacturing centre, but, taken as a whole, this pottery has exact counterparts in that found in Jewish tombs of the first century A.D. in the Jerusalem area, in the soundings against the north wall of Jerusalem (the dates of these have been established by coins of the Procurators and Agrippa I), and finally in the excavations of Herodian Jericho.[2]

Once this is accepted as the general date, we can attempt to determine the beginning and the end of the period involved. As we have seen, the few coins of Herod the Great[3] are very probably later in date than the destruction of Period I*b* and the ensuing abandonment, but it does not necessarily follow from

---

(not quoted by the author). In any case it would be necessary to look for more modest parallels, for example the private library containing the main stock of the papyri found at Herculaneum was a small room in which about 800 scrolls (cf. E. R. Barker, *Buried Herculaneum* (1908), 117) were piled up on shelves which were placed in the centre of the room and were the height of a man. Cf. in general C. Wendel, 'Bibliothek' in *Reallexikon für Antike und Christentum*, II (1954), 231–74, with bibliography; Ch. Callmer, 'Antike Bibliotheken', *Opuscula Archaeologica*, III (1944), 145–93, especially 155–6, on Herculaneum, and 189 n. 1, on the *armaria*, cupboards for books in private libraries, to which the wall cupboards in locs. 2 and 4 can be compared.

[1] Cf. p. 17.

[2] The references have been given in *Revue biblique*, LX (1953), 94; LXI (1954), 217; LXIII (1956), 551. On Herodian Jericho, cf. in addition to these J. B. Pritchard, 'The Excavations at Herodian Jericho', *The Annual of the American Schools of Oriental Research*, XXXII–XXXIII (1958). The parallels could be multiplied from examples given by Paul Lapp, *Palestinian Ceramic Chronology, 200 B.C.–A.D. 70*, 1961. The pottery of Qumran now appears less 'autonomous' or 'original' than I stated it to be at an earlier stage.

[3] Cf. pp. 22–3.

this that the resettlement—the beginning of Period II—would have taken place before the end of Herod's reign. His coins continued in circulation after his death, and this reoccupation could have taken place under his successor Herod Archelaus. Sixteen of this ruler's coins have in fact been recovered. From this point onwards the numismatic sequence of Period II continues uninterrupted. It includes 91 coins of the Procurators (33 of which were struck under Nero) and 78 coins of Agrippa I, and continues until the important group of coins belonging to the First Revolt, to which we shall return in order to determine the end of the period.

A further and important piece of evidence from the coin finds must also be taken into account. In addition to the coins which we are about to enumerate we discovered in loc. 120 a hoard of 561 pieces of silver preserved in three pots containing respectively 223, 185, and 153 pieces.[1] Two of these vessels are of a type which is foreign to those found at Qumran. They are small pots with large mouths and without handles, completely filled with coins, and with their mouths closed with a stopper of palm fibre. By contrast the third vessel was one of the juglets in common use at Khirbet Qumran, and, since its neck was too narrow for the pieces of silver to be dropped in through it, they were inserted by means of a hole which either already existed or which was specially made in the belly of the vessel. These three pots were buried beneath the level of Period II and above that of Period I*b*. An analysis of the hoard, therefore, can provide one piece of evidence by which the two periods can be chronologically distinguished. Each of these three collections is identical in composition, and the treasure can be considered as comprising a single hoard. With a few exceptions it includes only Tyrian coins, and these are almost exclusively tetradrachmae. Certain pieces go back to the last monarchs of the Seleucid dynasty, but the majority belong to the autonomous currency of Tyre, and the period when this was in use begins in 126 B.C. The later one proceeds in the period the more frequently all the various issues are represented, and the larger the number of new types. The most recent coin in the hoard is a tetradrachm from the year 118 of Tyre (9/8 B.C.) and several earlier pieces have been

[1] Cf. *Revue biblique*, LXIII (1956), 567–8.

countermarked in this same year. But this date provides only a *terminus post quem* for the burial of the hoard, because in the currency of Tyre a relative lacuna in the issues of new coins follows after the year 118, and it is not until the year 126 (1 B.C./A.D. 1) that new issues reappear in any quantity. Now in a hoard as representative as this the new issues would certainly have been included had it been amassed after that date.[1]

The treasure was therefore buried between 9/8 B.C. and 1 B.C./A.D. 1. As for its origin, two hypotheses may be put forward: either it was hidden in the ruins during the time when the site was abandoned between Periods I*b* and II, or else it was brought in and put in a safe place at the beginning of Period II. If the first hypothesis is correct, then this would imply that the building remained in a ruined condition at least up to 9/8 B.C. If the second is correct then this would mean that the building had been reoccupied, or was in process of being so, in 1 B.C./A.D. 1 at the latest.

A final discovery of coins may perhaps allow us to establish the date still more precisely. In Trench A was discovered part of the rubble cleared out of the buildings at the time of the re-installation.[2] The coins which were found in this rubble, and which have been identified, are the following: a silver tetradrachm of Antiochus VII Euergetes struck at Tyre in 131/130 B.C., a tetradrachm of autonomous Tyrian currency which is certainly earlier than our era but the date of which is illegible, an undated bronze of Antiochus III, an undated bronze of

---

[1] For information on these points I am indebted to M. H. Seyrig, who has most willingly undertaken a preliminary examination of the hoard. On 12 May 1955 he wrote to me as follows: 'With regard to the date of burial the crucial piece is the tetradrachm—unique until now—of the year 118 of Tyre (9/8 B.C.). But this date is only approximate, for this year 118 is followed by an unwonted gap in the issues of coins. Up to the present no silver coins are known of from the years 119–122 nor from 124, while 123 and 125 are known to me only by a single example from each. It is not until 126 that issues were once more struck in any quantity, and there would certainly have been representatives of these in the hoard if it had been buried after this date. It follows that the burial must have taken place towards 126 at the latest (1 B.C./A.D. 1).' There is another tetradrachm from the year 118 of Tyre in the small treasure of Jerusalem, an account of which has been published by G. F. Hill, *Quarterly of the Department of Antiquities in Palestine*, VI (1938), 78–83, and, although the sequence of coins in this hoard is fairly continuous this one is followed by a gap until the year 127.   [2] Cf. p. 25.

Antiochus IV, nineteen coins of Alexander Jannaeus, one coin of Hyrcanus II. All this fits well into Period I*b* and accords with the dates which we have assigned to it. The absence of coins of Herod the Great will also be noticed. There is only one coin which does not fit into this hypothesis: it is a coin of Herod Archelaus. It is reasonable to suppose that this was lost during the work of clearance.

Herod Archelaus reigned from 4 B.C. to A.D. 6. If the reoccupation took place during the first years of his reign this date would fit in well with the hoard of silver coins which was buried at latest in 1 B.C./A.D. 1, and would justify us in assigning to Period II certain coins of Herod the Great which are more recent, and which would have been brought in by those who reoccupied the settlement. The probable conclusion is, therefore, that the beginning of Period II falls at the outset of the reign of Herod Archelaus, between 4 and 1 B.C.

The end of Period II is marked by a violent destruction. In the main building the tower to the north-west, fortified by its ramp of stones, offered a stouter resistance. But all the rooms of the south-west and north-west were filled with debris from the collapse of the ceilings and superstructures to a height which varies between 1·10 m. and 1·50 m. In the centre and the south-east, where the courtyard is situated and certain lighter structures had been put up, the damage was less considerable, but the destruction extended throughout the whole building. Iron arrow-heads have been recovered, and almost everywhere a layer of a powdery black substance gives evidence of the burning of the roofs. The buildings, therefore, were reduced to ruins by a military action, and, since the last coins of Period II are Jewish coins from the First Revolt, it is reasonable to conclude that the destruction took place during the Jewish War.[1] This lasted from A.D. 66 to 70, when Jerusalem was captured, or up to 73 if we include in it the resistance and the fall of Masada, the scene of the final stand.

Here too evidence is available for attempting to determine the

[1] The carbon-14 dating is too imprecise to be useful here. However, I may point out that the experiments made on fragments of beams of palm wood coming from loc. 86 indicate that they were burned about A.D. 66. Cf. F. E. Zeuner, 'Notes on Qumrân', *Palestine Exploration Quarterly*, 1960, 27–8.

precise date. There are 94 coins, all of bronze, from the First Revolt, and of these 83 belong to the second year, 5 to the third, and 6 are too oxidized for us to decide whether they belong to the second or the third year. Most of them were discovered in two groups. Outside the building, against the western containing wall, loc. 103, there was a collection of 39 coins which had become stuck together through the process of oxidization. They must have been held together in a bag, though the material of this has perished. This was a small hoard abandoned in the moment of the destruction. From a decantation basin, loc. 83, 33 coins of the First Revolt have been recovered, and in addition one coin of the Procurators, one of Agrippa I, and one silver coin struck at Antioch under Nero in A.D. 62/63. These pieces were intermingled with the debris and with sherds which had been thrown into this basin at the time when the new occupants of Period III cleared out part of the ruins so as to establish themselves there. The bronzes of the third year of the First Revolt are less frequent than those of the second year, but one of the types of the fourth year is particularly common.[1] These bronzes from the fourth year would certainly have been represented at Qumran if the occupation had been prolonged up to the date when they were struck.[2] It seems, then, that the destruction must have taken place in the third year of the rebellion, A.D. 68/69. This conclusion seems to be confirmed by the coins belonging to the following period. They have been discovered in the level of reconstruction extending above the ruins of Period II, which show a very clear alteration in the plan and function of the buildings. This is Period III. Now the earliest coins to which a precise date can be assigned, and which certainly derive from this Period III,[3] are 9 of Caesarea from the reign of Nero dated A.D. 67/68, and 4 from the same year struck at Dora,

[1] Cf. L. Kadman, *The Coins of the Jewish War of 66–73 C.E.* (*Corpus Nummorum Palaestinensium*, Ser. 2, vol. III), 1960, 72–8.

[2] Hence it is that at Masada, which remained in the hands of the Jews, a number of coins of the Revolt have been found, including the last issue of silver shekels from the fifth year of that Revolt, *Revue biblique*, LXXIII (1966), 233 with references.

[3] Certainly there is a Tyrian coin from A.D. 53/54, but this has been found on the top of loc. 40 in a lamp which also contained a coin of Caesarea of A.D. 67/68. These must be taken together in our estimates, and it is the most recent in date which is significant.

near Caesarea. These coins represent more than half the total number of coins attributable to Period III.

Now let us return to the two groups of coins belonging to the First Revolt. The first contains 37 pieces from the second year, A.D. 67/68, and two pieces from the third year, A.D. 68/69. The other contains 31 pieces from the second year and 2 pieces from the third year. This third year began, according to the Jewish computation, in Nisan (March–April) 68.[1] Now a little after this date the Roman armies were active in the region of Jericho.[2] We know of the dispositions of the troops from Josephus' *Jewish War*. Caesarea remained the principal base right up to the siege of Jerusalem (apart from the references which follow, cf. *Bell.* III. ix. 409, 443, 446; IV. iii. 130; vii. 419; xi. 663; v. i. 40). During the year 67 Vespasian left the Fifth and Tenth legions at Caesarea to take up their winter quarters there, and sent the Fifteenth to Scythopolis, III. ix. 412.[3] Shortly afterwards the

[1] This has been contested by C. Roth, *Palestine Exploration Quarterly*, 1959, 128–9: the Revolt having begun in the autumn of 66, the third year would only have commenced in the autumn of 68, and these coins from the third year prove, so he alleges, that Khirbet Qumran was not destroyed by the Romans in June 68 as I have stated and as I shall reiterate here. It is true that in Josephus' computation the years of the Revolt are taken to begin from the autumn of 66. Thus *Bell.* IV. ix. 577, the taking of Jerusalem by Simon Bar Giora in Xanthicus (= Nisan) 69 is likewise 'dated in the third year of the war' but the coins followed the calendar beginning in the spring. Cf. G. F. Hill, *A Catalogue of the Greek Coins in the British Museum*, Palestine, 1914, p. xci; B. Kanael, *Bulletin of the American Schools of Oriental Research*, **129** (Feb. 1953), 19 n. 8. L. Kadman, 'The Coinage of the Jewish Roman War', *loc. cit.*, p. 44. There are silver shekels from the year V. They would not have been in existence if the years had been counted as beginning from the autumn of 66, Jerusalem having been taken in September 70. More recently, in his article, 'The Year-Reckoning of the Coins of the First Revolt', *Numismatic Chronicle*, ser. VII. ii (1962), 91–100, C. Roth suggests May 68 as the beginning of the third year according to a calendar of the rebels which would have taken as its starting-point May–June 66. But he considers that this does not make any difference to his conclusions, in which he is opposed to the idea of a destruction of Qumran in June 68.

[2] I am developing what I have already stated in *Revue biblique*, LXI (1954), 232–3; LXIII (1956), 567; LXVI (1959), 100, and revising it so as to take into account the observations of F. M. Cross, *The Ancient Library of Qumran and Modern Biblical Studies*, 2nd edn., 1961, pp. 61–3; C. Roth, 'Did Vespasian Capture Qumran?', *Palestine Exploration Quarterly*, 1959, 122–9.

[3] In order to reconcile this piece of information with that of IV. ii. 87, in which the Tenth legion is said to be stationed at Scythopolis, F. M. Cross

legions at Caesarea were summoned to Scythopolis, and the three legions marched upon Taricheae, which they forced to surrender, III. ix. 446–61. After this the three legions took part in the siege of Gamala in October–November 67, IV. i. 13, 83. After the fall of this city Vespasian summoned the Tenth legion to Scythopolis and brought back the other two to Caesarea, IV. ii. 87–8. At the beginning of the spring of 68 Vespasian transferred the greater part of his troops from Caesarea to Antipatris, reduced the region to submission, and established the Fifth legion at Emmaus, IV. viii. 443–5. With the remainder of his troops he campaigned as far as Idumaea and returned to Emmaus. From there he passed near Nablus and descended by Wadi Far'ah to Coreae in the Jordan valley, arriving there in the second fortnight of June. One day later he was at Jericho. The majority of the inhabitants had fled. The rest were massacred. At Jericho Vespasian was joined by Trajan who brought him the troops stationed at Perea, IV. viii. 446–51. This Trajan, the father of the future emperor, was the legate of the Tenth legion, III. vii. 289. It is likely, therefore, that the troops which had been campaigning in the Perea from March 68 onwards under the orders of the tribune Placidus, IV. vii. 414, 419, and which Trajan brought to Jericho, belonged to this Tenth legion.[1] Vespasian set up a permanent camp at Jericho, IV. ix. 486, and we may conjecture that this was occupied by the Tenth legion, for it was from Jericho that Titus brought it up in the year 70 for the siege of Jerusalem.[2] After the occupation of Jericho

suggests correcting IV. ix. 412. But this correction is unnecessary, since a change could have taken place after the episode of Gamala.

[1] Thus F. M. Cross, *loc. cit.*, and C. Roth, *Journal of Theological Studies*, N.S. x (1959), p. 92. But in *Palestine Exploration Quarterly, loc. cit.*, this latter author states that he has not found any proof that the Tenth legion ever left Galilee between 67 and 70. All the same we do have here the name of its commander and a mention of Jericho in connection with the Tenth legion. Cf. the note following.

[2] *Bell.* v. i. 42; ii. 69. It is true that in the two cases the text reads διὰ Ἰεριχοῦντος and that one could translate (thus C. Roth) 'passing through Jericho', the point of departure being more distant. But in the first passage the movement of the Tenth legion διὰ Ἰεριχοῦντος is parallel to that of the Fifth legion δι' Ἀμμαοῦς. Now we have seen that the Fifth legion was stationed at Emmaus, cf. also v. ii. 67. In the second passage the mention of Jericho is followed by the phrase 'where a small part of the regular army was stationed guarding the pass', cf. IV. ix. 486. The meaning of this remark is clear

Vespasian remained in the city only a short time, for he was back again at Caesarea when he learned of the death of Nero, IV. ix. 491. This event took place on 9 June 68 and the news would not have taken very long to reach Palestine. During this brief stay at Jericho Vespasian advanced to the shores of the Dead Sea, and in order to verify the report that it was difficult to sink in it he had some men thrown into it who could not swim and who had their hands tied behind their backs. All of them floated, IV. viii. 477. It is true that Josephus does not mention any military action to the south of Jericho, but no argument can be adduced from his silence on this point, for it is conceivable that a minor episode, such as the destruction of Khirbet Qumran would have been, was not recorded in the sources upon which he drew. Whatever the particular movements of each legion,[1] and whatever the nature of Vespasian's expedition to the shores of the Dead Sea, whether for war or sight-seeing, the fact remains that in June 68 some Roman troops which had been staying at Caesarea in the course of the preceding year occupied Jericho, that in the same month their leader came to the shores of the Dead Sea, and that from this date onwards the region remained in subjection to the Romans. Thereafter it ceased to be the scene of any military operation. After the fall of Jerusalem only three strongholds remained in the hands of the insurgents: the Herodium and Machaerus which were taken by Lucilius Bassus, and Masada which fell in A.D. 73 after a bitter siege

provided this troop is in fact the Tenth legion. It must be understood that the Tenth legion goes up 'by Jericho' where its camp was situated just as the Fifth legion goes up 'by Emmaus' where its camp lay. At least this is the way in which historians have understood the matter up to the present. Cf. E. Schürer, *Geschichte des jüdischen Volkes*, I⁵ (1920), 625; Ganschinietz, 'Legio (Xᵃ Fretensis)' in Pauly–Wissowa, *Real-Encyclopädie* ..., XII. ii (1925), 1673; F. M. Abel, *Histoire de la Palestine depuis la conquête d'Alexandre jusqu'à l'invasion arabe*, II, 1952, p. 19.

[1] Recent discussions refer to the existence of a coin with the countersign of the Tenth legion, which, so it is held, was found at Khirbet Qumran and which I have in fact recorded, *Revue biblique*, LXI (1954), 230, 233, and again LXVI (1959), 100. The mention of this was unfortunate for this coin does not exist. Faced with a coin which was incomplete and much oxidized I believed that I could read the remains of an X, the countersign of the Tenth legion. But Fr. Spijkerman has convinced me that it is the cruciform mark which appears on the stern of a galley in the designs of the coins of Ashkelon of A.D. 72/73. Cf. G. F. Hill, *A Catalogue ... Palestine*, p. 112, no. 46 and pl. xiii, I.

under the leadership of Flavius Silva. To link the destruction of Khirbet Qumran with one or other of these remote and restricted actions is a conjecture without any basis either in archaeology or in the literary sources.

Thus the evidence of history agrees with that of the coinage. It is perfectly true that strictly speaking the coins only provide a *terminus post quem*. It is also true that the numismatic sequence emerging from an excavation may have, and in fact generally does have, certain lacunae. Thus the Jewish coins, the last of which were put into circulation in Nisan A.D. 68, do not prove *per se* that the Jews must have left Khirbet Qumran in 68. The Roman coins which begin in A.D. 67/68 do not *per se* prove that the Romans installed themselves at Khirbet Qumran in this same year, 68. But since these two groups of coins are distributed precisely between two successive levels, the Jewish coins certainly belonging to the lower level, that of the destruction, and the Roman coins certainly belonging to the level above this, the level of the reconstruction, it is reasonable to put forward the hypothesis that the year 68, at which the two numismatic sequences meet, marks the destruction of the lower level and the initiation of the higher one. And, since this explanation is in accordance with the historical data, it acquires that degree of certainty with which a historian of antiquity often has to be content. It is in this sense that I consider it certain that Khirbet Qumran was destroyed by the Romans in June 68 of our era.[1]

V. PERIOD III

The destruction of Khirbet Qumran will therefore have been at the hands of Roman soldiers, whose arrow-heads have been found there as well as certain of the coins which they had received in their pay, the coins of Caesarea (and of Dora nearby), where they were stationed in the course of the year A.D. 67/68. However, these coins were not lost during the attack on the building for they were not found in the layer of destruction.

---

[1] This argument has not convinced everyone. Cf. in particular the criticisms of G. R. Driver, *The Judaean Scrolls. The Problem and a Solution*, 1965, 394–6, and J. L. Teicher, *Antiquity*, xxxvii (1963), 25–30. I have replied to Driver in *Revue biblique*, LXXIII (1966), 232–4, and to Teicher in *Antiquity*, xxxvii, 126–7.

They were in the level of reconstruction, which implies that a small military post was left on the site. This measure is to be explained by the continuing need for the Romans to keep watch on the shores of the Dead Sea. From the plateau of Qumran the view extends over the whole of the western shore from the mouth of the Jordan to Ras Feshkha and över the whole southern half of the sea. This watch was made necessary by the military operations which followed. After the fall of Jerusalem and the surrender of the Herodium and Machaerus the Jews still held the fortress of Masada, which overlooked the Dead Sea 45 kilometres to the south of Khirbet Qumran. This did not fall until April of A.D. 73.[1] Moreover, Flavius Silva had committed a large army to the siege, and consequently needed to see that his lines of supply and contact were secure. Certainly in order to reach Masada there are easier routes than that which leads by way of Khirbet Qumran and 'Ain Feshkha, but it is possible that apart from the land routes the Romans would also have made use of boats. They had already had experience of navigation on the lake in 68 when they used boats to pursue the Jews of the Perea who were trying to escape by sea.[2] At all events the Romans would have had to patrol the sea and its shores right up to the end of the campaign. It is this that explains the new character which Khirbet Qumran acquires in Period III (Pl. XXIII).[3] Only one part of the ruins was reoccupied. In the main building the large tower was re-utilized, the wall extending eastwards from it was doubled in thickness, and the rooms on the north-east were slightly altered. To the south of the tower the thick layer of destruction was levelled out and the well-ordered plan of Period II was replaced by a group of small rooms juxtaposed without any particular order. It is in these two regions that all the coins except two of Period III have been found. The south-eastern quarter of the main building was not reoccupied. Since it was suitable for use as a military post the defences were strengthened. The extra thickness added to the north wall has already been noticed, and in addition the central court of the old building was shut off by a large wall. The gaps in the south

---

[1] *Bell.* VII. ix. 401.
[2] *Ibid.*, IV. vii. 439.
[3] Cf. *Revue biblique*, LXI (1954), 213–14; LXIII (1956), 547–8.

front were closed and a ditch was dug along the western wall. The entire western part of the Khirbeh was left in ruins.

The Romans cleared out part of the debris encumbering the area which they used. That in the chambers on the north-eastern side was thrown outside the building and, as one would expect, the archaeological evidence from this debris appears in inverse order, and the coins of Period I*b* found there are above those of Period II. The debris cleared out of the rooms on the southern side was thrown into neighbouring cisterns. The debris covered the bottom of cistern 56, formed mounds at the north-west corner and against the eastern side of cistern 58 (Pl. xxiv*a*), filled the decantation basin at 83, and blocked the steps at the entrance of the large cistern on the south-western side, loc. 85.

The effect was that major changes were introduced into the arrangements for the water supply. It would have been necessary to carry out major repairs to the complex water system of Period II. Constant maintenance work would have been required and it would have been out of all proportion to the needs of the little garrison. The Romans kept only the large cistern to the south-east, loc. 71, which had suffered least damage, being more isolated from the buildings. The system of channels was greatly simplified. The large reservoir to the south-west, loc. 91, was filled in with debris coming from the building and also with earth, some of it from the defensive ditch and probably also some taken from the large pits which were dug at the time in the rooms nearby, locs. 102, 104. Once the cistern had been filled in in this way a new and poorly constructed channel was built over it to connect with the old channel in loc. 100 (Pl. xxiv*b*). It cut across the cistern at 91 and then across the annexe to the assembly room, loc. 86, ran along the outside of this room, and finished its course by rejoining the old channel near loc. 72.

It will be seen that all this constitutes a radical transformation. There are no longer any places of collective assembly or any workshops, and the potter's kiln now serves as a store for lime. For the needs of this small group there is only one bread oven set up above the ruins at the foot of the tower. This is visible in Pl. xxiii. In contrast to the continuity which we have remarked between Periods I*b* and II, Period III marks an open break. Community life at Qumran no longer exists. It ceased in A.D. 68.

Apart from the coins there are few objects to illustrate the life of this period. In contrast to the plentiful harvest of the lower levels, there is a scarcity of pottery.[1] Those forms of Period II for which abundant parallels exist in other sites of the first century A.D. are again to be met with here, but there is a marked absence of the types which are peculiar to Khirbet Qumran itself. The potter's workshop had ceased to function and the ceramics of Period III bear witness to an essentially limited occupation following immediately upon Period II, but different in kind and only of brief duration.

We do not know exactly when this occupation ended. Apart from the group of coins of A.D. 67/68 which have already been mentioned, Period III is documented by one undated coin from Antioch of the reign of Nero, earlier therefore than A.D. 68, one coin with the names of Claudia, Nero's daughter and Poppaea his wife, who were deified[2] (this belongs to A.D. 65 at the earliest), one silver coin from Antioch of the reign of Vespasian and Titus in 69/70, two coins from Ashkelon of A.D. 72/73, four coins of *Judaea Capta* ascribed to Titus which are of uncertain date.[3] Finally there is one coin of Agrippa II from the year A.D. 87, but this was found outside the building and its attribution to Period III is doubtful. The possibility cannot be excluded that the military occupation lasted at least up to this date, but in that case it is difficult to explain the fact that no Palestinian issue is represented which falls between the coins of Ashkelon of A.D. 72/73 (and also the coins of *Judaea Capta* if these are not later) and the single coin of Agrippa II.[4] Merely from the coins found at Qumran, therefore, it can be concluded with a certain degree of probability that following upon the fall of Masada in A.D. 73 the military outpost was suppressed. We shall see whether the discoveries at Feshkha agree with this conclusion.[5]

[1] *Revue biblique*, LXI (1954), 217.

[2] This is the coin described by F. de Saulcy, *Numismatique de la Terre Sainte*, 1874, p. 314. The attribution of this to Panias is a conjecture.

[3] In *Revue biblique*, LXVI (1959), 101, n. 2, I said that these coins must be later than the accession of Titus as emperor in A.D. 79. This is not certain. The coins of *Judaea Capta* struck in Palestine are undated, but coins of the same type in the name of Titus were struck at Rome from A.D. 72 onwards. The coins at Qumran could be equally old.

[4] Cf. B. Kanael, 'Some Observations on the Chronology of Khirbet Qumran', *Eretz-Israel*, v (1958), 169 (in Hebrew).   [5] Cf. pp. 70–1.

VI. THE SECOND REVOLT

The abandoned buildings were used either as a hiding place or as a centre of resistance by the insurgents of the Second Jewish Revolt in A.D. 132–5. No actual building work can be attributed to them except perhaps a wall dividing the old cistern at 58 in two, which has been built above the rubble left from Period III, and also a natural deposit later than this accumulation of debris.[1] But several of the coins belonging to these insurgents have been found. One of these[2] was in an isolated position in the upper layer of the main building. But in a room on the ground floor of the tower which still remained accessible, the bottom of a bowl had been buried containing ten coins: five bronze coins, one silver denarius of the Second Revolt, one denarius of Vespasian, three denarii of Trajan. Among these coins of the Second Revolt some belong to the second year while others are undated. If, as seems to have been demonstrated,[3] these undated coins are the most recent in the sequence, the occupation of Khirbet Qumran belongs to the end of the war, and to that stage in it where the insurgents, hunted down by the Roman legions, sought refuge in the desert of Judaea, as we have learned from discoveries made in the caves of Murabba'at.[4]

This was only one brief episode, and the final one in the history of Khirbet Qumran. The few surface finds of coins, the dates of which extend from the third century A.D. to the Turkish period, indicate nothing more than the passing of chance travellers.

VII. THE CEMETERY

To the east of the ruins, and separated from them by an empty space of nearly fifty metres, extends a vast cemetery containing

[1] *Revue biblique*, LXIII (1956), 548.

[2] And not three as was stated in *Revue biblique*, LXI (1954), 230 and 233; LXIII (1956), 567.

[3] A. Kindler, 'The Coinage of the Bar-Kokhbar War', in *The Dating and Meaning of Ancient Jewish Coins and Symbols, loc. cit.*, 71–3.

[4] Cf. R. de Vaux, 'Les grottes de Murabba'ât et leurs documents', *Revue biblique*, LX (1953), 245–67, and especially P. Benoit, J. T. Milik, R. de Vaux, Discoveries in the Judaean Desert, II, *Les Grottes de Murabba'ât*, (1961).

about 1,100 tombs.[1] It takes up all the rest of the plateau and the tombs are arranged in regular and closely ordered rows divided into three areas separated by alleys. This careful ordering is in contrast to the disorder usual in the ancient cemeteries of Palestine. The tombs are marked by oval-shaped heaps of stones appearing on the surface, often with a larger stone at either end (Pl. xxv*a*). They are all orientated from north to south except one which points from east to west. Twenty-six of these tombs have been excavated, selected from the different sectors. They conform to a type which is constant throughout: beneath the oval heap of stones a rectangular cavity has been dug out in the gravelly surface and then in the firmer marl of the plateau to a depth which varies between 1·20 m. and 2 m. At the bottom of this cavity the loculus has been dug, almost always sideways under the eastern wall of the cavity. This is closed sometimes by mud bricks (Pl. xxvi*a*) and sometimes by flat stones (Pl. xxv*b*), the chinks being filled in with earth. Apart from one instance where two bodies have been laid side by side in the same loculus, they are individual tombs. The skeleton lies stretched out on its back, the head to the south (except in one case), the hands folded on the pelvis or stretched alongside the body (Pl. xxvi*b*). There is one instance of re-inhumation. In a loculus of the same type as the others the incomplete bones of two individuals have been found arranged in two separate piles. Furthermore, at the western extremity of the cemetery a group of three tombs of a slightly different type has been excavated. These were marked by a circle of stones and, at the bottom of one trench, once more orientated from north to south but not quite in accordance with the usual form, there were found, under a covering of slabs or mud bricks, the remains of a wooden coffin in which the body had been laid in the dorsal position. Another tomb, likewise on the edge of the cemetery, consisted of a rectangular trench which was broader and shallower than in the general run of the tombs. The skeleton in it was lying on its back, its head to the south, the left hand on the pelvis and the right on the chest.

This cemetery extends over the low hills sloping downwards to the east of the plateau. The position of the tombs here is far

[1] *Revue biblique*, LX (1953), 95 and 102–3; LXI (1954), 207; LXIII (1956), 569–72.

less regular, and their orientation is not constant. Seven of these tombs have been excavated. Two of these were irregular trenches where the bones of an individual had been re-buried. In two others a brown dust bore witness to the fact that there the body had been buried in a wooden coffin.

Apart from some instances which are uncertain due to the bad state of preservation of the bones, all the skeletons in that part of the cemetery which is carefully planned are male. The same is true of those in the tombs beneath a circle of stones on the western extremity of the cemetery. Only the rectangular grave, which is abnormal in type and situated apart from the rows, contained a female skeleton. By contrast, in the extensions of the cemetery over the hillocks to the east four of the six skeletons examined are of women while one is of a child. All these men and women died young, and very few had passed their fortieth year. The indications as to sex and age are useful, but the small number of the tombs excavated does not permit us to draw any statistics from them which can validly be applied to the cemetery as a whole.

Apart from a few rare ornaments, beads and earrings found near the two female skeletons, the tombs did not contain any objects laid next to the body. Nevertheless, it is certain that these tombs—apart perhaps from those which are anomalous in type —are contemporaneous with the community settlement at Khirbet Qumran. Few sherds were embodied in the mud bricks or mixed with the earth used to fill in the tombs above the loculus, but such as there were are identical with those which have been recovered from the ruins. In two cases the evidence is still more clear. The filling of a tomb contained fragments of a jar of Period I*b* while that of another tomb contained intact a lamp of Period II.

In April 1966 S. H. Steckoll excavated a tomb in the main part of the cemetery. It was of the type described above and contained the skeleton of a man of more than sixty-five. Some stones placed near the head and thorax had been inscribed with a 'funeral-text', 'which was revealed only . . . under ultra-violet light'.[1]

---

[1] S. H. Steckoll, 'Preliminary Excavation Report in the Qumran Cemetery', *Revue de Qumran*, vi. 3 (1968), 323–44; N. Haas–H. Nathan, 'Anthropological Survey of the Human Skeletal Remains from Qumran', *ibid.*, 345–52.

No other details have been supplied about this discovery, which must be regarded as suspect. In December 1966 and March 1967 S. H. Steckoll excavated eight other tombs (five of men, two of women, one of whom had been buried with a baby of two years old, and a little girl). Nothing has been published on these excavations apart from a brief note.[1] Deformation of the bones indicated that among these individuals there was a scribe, a horseman, a man who walked barefoot, and a labourer who carried heavy weights on his shoulders. The authorities of the Israeli occupation have forbidden this Sherlock Holmes of archaeology to continue his researches at Qumran.

The historical periods of Khirbet Qumran which archaeology enables us to distinguish are not all of equal importance. The Israelite settlement is only a preamble concerning which we are ill-informed. The occupation by the Roman soldiers and the utilization of the ruins by the insurgents of the Second Jewish Revolt are only secondary episodes. The essential fact is the communal occupation of Periods I and II. A group of men came to Khirbet Qumran and installed themselves there in the second half of the second century B.C., Period I*a*. The buildings were very quickly extended and assumed what is more or less their definitive form, Period I*b*. In 31 B.C. an earthquake damaged the buildings which afterwards remained abandoned up to the years just before and just after the beginning of the Christian era. They were then reoccupied by the same community, Period II, and survived until A.D. 68, when they were destroyed by the Roman army.

The principal characteristic of the buildings at Qumran is the fact that they were designed for community living and the fact that elements intended for collective use preponderate so greatly over those which could have served as dwelling-quarters. On the other hand the number of the tombs in the cemetery is too high in relation to the number of inhabitants which the buildings could have accommodated and the length of time during which they were occupied. The explanation of these anomalies will become apparent when we move on to study the archaeological remains discovered in the region near Khirbet Qumran.

[1] In the article cited in the preceding note, pp. 335–6.

II

THE ARCHAEOLOGY OF THE AREA
SURROUNDING QUMRAN

THE area surrounding Khirbet Qumran has become famous as a result of the ancient manuscripts found there, and it was in fact the discovery of the first scrolls in a cave nearby that drew the archaeologists' attention to the site. Fresh discoveries made it necessary to broaden the field of their explorations so as to include the whole of the terrain extending northwards and southwards from Khirbet Qumran, and we have now to present the archaeological findings which arise from this work.

I. THE FIRST CAVE

The cave in which the Bedouin found the first manuscripts was identified by an officer of the Arab Legion, and from 15 February to 5 March 1949 it was excavated by the Jordanian Department of Antiquities, the Palestine Archaeological Museum, and the École Archéologique Française de Jérusalem.[1] It is a little over 1 km. distant from Khirbet Qumran in a cleft fairly high up in the rocky cliffs (Pl. xxviia). It is a simple natural crevice in the rock, 8 m. long, 4 m. high, and varying in breadth from 0·75 m. to 2 m. (Cave 1Q). In addition to the manuscripts taken out by the Bedouin and the very large quantity of fragments collected by the excavators it contained numerous scraps of cloth, fragments of wood, olive- and date-stones, palm fibre, leather phylactery cases, and a mass of broken pottery.

This pottery comprises a number of the characteristic cylindrical jars (Pl. xxiib) and lids, but also three bowls, a pot, a juglet, two lamps conforming to Hellenistic types, and two lamps of the Roman period. All the ceramic material has its exact

---

[1] *Revue biblique*, LVI (1949), 234–7; 586–609; D. Barthélemy and J. T. Milik, Discoveries in the Judaean Desert, I, *Qumran Cave I* (1955).

counterparts at Khirbet Qumran and the differences between the lamps indicate that examples from two distinct periods of the Khirbeh, I*b* and II, are represented here. None of the pieces is either earlier or later than the period of the communal occupation of the Khirbeh. The carbon-14 dating of the linen fabrics was A.D. 33, with a margin of error of 200 years on either side,[1] and a study by the late Mrs. Crowfoot of the actual weaves employed has shown that a date towards the end of the first century A.D. is highly probable.[2]

II. THE CAVES IN THE ROCK CLIFFS

In February 1962 the Bedouin found a fresh cave with manuscripts (Cave 2Q) between the first cave and Khirbet Qumran. All that they discovered were fragments, which were immediately sold, but the Palestine Archaeological Museum and the École Archéologique Française, this time in association with the American School of Oriental Research at Jerusalem, thereupon decided to undertake a systematic clearance of this cave, and also to explore all the rock cliffs throughout the Qumran region.[3] Cave 2Q is very irregular. The floor is uneven and it has small chambers or cavities at two different levels. It had been carefully emptied of its contents by the Bedouin. The spoil they had left contained fragments of a good half-dozen cylindrical jars, one lid, and three bowls. As in the case of the first cave, nothing is either earlier or later than the main phase of occupation at Khirbet Qumran.

A section of the cliffs about 8 km. long was explored, Khirbet Qumran lying roughly halfway between the two extremes. At this time a third cave with manuscripts was discovered (Cave 3Q), somewhat to the north of the first. It contained inscribed fragments of hide and papyrus and a copper scroll in two parts

[1] O. R. Sellers, 'Radiocarbon Dating of Cloths from the 'Aïn Feshkha Cave', *Bulletin of the American Schools of Oriental Research*, **123** (Oct. 1951), 24–6.

[2] In Discoveries in the Judaean Desert, i, 18–35, especially 27.

[3] W. L. Reed, 'The Qumran Caves Expedition of March, 1952', *Bulletin of the American Schools of Oriental Research*, **135** (Oct. 1954), 8–13; R. de Vaux, 'Exploration de la région de Qumrân', *Revue biblique*, LX (1953), 540–61; M. Baillet, J. T. Milik, R. de Vaux, Les *'Petites Grottes'* de Qumrân, Discoveries in the Judaean Desert, III (1962).

on which a long passage in Mishnaic Hebrew had been en-graved,[1] and, in addition, a large quantity of pottery: more than 30 cylindrical jars, more than 20 lids, 2 jugs, and a lamp.

But many other signs of occupation were discovered (Pl. XL). An exploration was made of the holes, caves, and crevices with which the cliffs are everywhere honeycombed. Of the soundings taken 230 proved barren, but 40 of these cavities contained pottery and other objects. These remains range in date from the Chalcolithic to the Arab period, but 26 of the sites explored yielded pottery which was identical with that of the first cave of Khirbet Qumran. It was not possible to make this exploration exhaustive. In September 1952 the Bedouin discovered a hole at the mouth of Wady Qumran (Cave 6Q) from which they took fragments of manuscript, a jar, and a bowl of the Qumran type.[2] In 1956, a little to the south of Cave 3Q, they opened up a cave (Cave 11Q), the entrance of which had become blocked, and took an important group of manuscripts from it. It was exca-vated by the three institutions working at Khirbet Qumran at the time (Pl. XXVIIb). This cave had been inhabited in the Chalcolithic period, in Iron Age II, and finally at the same period as Khirbet Qumran, as the pottery found there (but rare elsewhere) attests.[3]

The only caves with which we shall be concerned here are those containing ceramic material identical with that of Qum-ran. All of them have openings in the lower part of the cliffs and constitute natural cavities. The density of occupation increases

---

[1] Published by J. T. Milik in Discoveries in the Judaean Desert, III, 211–302. The studies to which this text has given rise have been analysed by H. Bardtke, *Theologische Rundschau*, N.F. XXXIII (1968), 185–204.

[2] Discoveries in the Judaean Desert, III, 10 and 26.

[3] *Revue biblique*, LXIII (1956), 573–4. Up to the present only a single manu-script of Cave 11 has been published, J. A. Sanders, *The Psalms Scroll of Qumran Cave 11*, Discoveries in the Judaean Desert, IV (1965); idem, *The Dead Sea Psalm Scroll* (1967). A fresh fragment has been published by Y. Yadin, 'Another Fragment (E) of the Psalms Scroll from Qumran Cave 11', *Textus*, V (1966), 1–10. On the Targum of Job: J. van der Ploeg, *Le Targum de Job de la grotte 11 de Qumran (11 Qtg Job). Première communication*, Mededelingen der Koninklijke Nederlandse Akademie van Wetenschappen, Afd. Letterkunde, n.r. xxv. 9 (1962). It is possible, though not certain, that Cave 11 was also the place where the major manuscript confiscated by the Israelis during the Six Days' War was discovered in 1967. It is now known as the 'Temple Scroll'.

in the vicinity of Khirbet Qumran. Elsewhere it is noticeable
that there are points at which the sites are grouped together and
also long stretches where they are completely absent. This can
be explained either by variations of contour in the terrain or by
the greater ease of access at these particular points. The pottery
is abundant (Pl. xxix). It consists chiefly of cylindrical jars and
lids, and while some variants can undoubtedly be distinguished
among them, they conform consistently to the types characteristic of Khirbet Qumran. Other forms are scarce: a few bowls,
jugs, juglets, lamps, and a plate, all of forms which have their
counterparts at Khirbet Qumran (Pl. xlii).

III. THE CAVES IN THE MARL TERRACE

During this exploration we restricted our research to the rock
cliffs and did not examine the marl terrace stretching in front of
them. The reason was that the nature of the terrain is such as to
exclude in this marl terrace the presence of any natural caves
suitable for human use. All that we noticed were cavities eroded
by water which were archaeologically barren. In this we erred.
Six months after we had left the Bedouin returned, and discovered a cave artificially hollowed out in the marl terrace and
containing an immense number of manuscript fragments (Cave
4Q). It was situated on the other side of the ravine bounding
the esplanade of Qumran to the west and just opposite to it
(Pl. xxviii). It comprised an oval chamber opening on to two
smaller chambers which had been partially eroded away. The
Jordanian Department of Antiquities put a stop to the clandestine excavation and, together with representatives of the Palestine Archaeological Museum and the École Archéologique
Française, immediately went to the cave to clear it completely
and subject it to close examination. This lasted from 22 to
29 September 1952. Numerous fragments of manuscript were
again recovered here, but there was relatively little pottery:
parts of several jars, several lids, several bowls, two jugs, a pot,
a juglet, and a lamp, all belonging to the period of community
life at Khirbet Qumran.[1]

[1] Provisionally in *Revue biblique*, lx (1953), 86. Apart from the preliminary
publication of a fairly large number of fragments, only a single volume has

Then, just to the north of Cave 4Q, another cave was recognized (Cave 5Q) and excavated from 25 to 28 September. It consisted of a simple chamber with rounded corners (Pl. xxvIII). Fragments of manuscript had been preserved in it, but not a single sherd of pottery nor any other ancient object.[1]

During the campaign of 1955 at Khirbet Qumran, and from 7 February to 15 March of the same year, a team of workmen made a comprehensive examination of the flanks surrounding the marl terrace of Khirbet Qumran, extending this along Wadi Qumran as far as the rock cliffs.[2] At the end of the esplanade extending southwards from the ruins it was possible to discern traces where there had once been three further caves (that is Caves 7Q, 8Q, 9Q), though the greater part of them had been carried away by landslides or erosion. However, some remains had been preserved in them: fragments of manuscript, phylactery cases, date-stones, the ends of pieces of material or ropes, scraps of leather, and a few pieces of pottery. The latter comprised, once more, cylindrical jars and lids, bowls, goblets, and lamps. On the west face of the spur in which Cave 4Q had been hollowed out half of another cave (Cave 10Q) had survived. Its floor was covered with a mat. Apart from an ostracon in Hebrew, it contained only date-stones and desiccated dates, the fragments of a lamp, and sherds of the general type of Qumran.

In contrast with the caves in the cliffs, all those in the marl terrace without exception were unquestionably chambers which had been artificially hollowed out, showing clear signs of having been the work of human hands.

IV. THE CONNECTION BETWEEN THE CAVES AND THE RUINS

We have seen that in most of the caves and hollows in the cliffs which had been put to human use pottery has survived

so far appeared of the definitive edition of the texts from Cave 4Q: J. M. Allegro, A. A. Anderson, *Qumran Cave 4, I (4Q 58–4Q 186)*, Discoveries in the Judaean Desert, v (1968). Cf. also the long and critical review article by J. Strugnell entitled 'Notes en marge du volume v des "Discoveries in the Judaean Desert of Jordan"', *Revue de Qumran*, vII (1970), 163–276.

[1] Discoveries in the Judaean Desert, III, 26.

[2] *Revue biblique*, LXIII (1956), 572–3; Discoveries in the Judaean Desert, III, 27–31.

belonging to the same types as at Khirbet Qumran. Moreover, in most cases it belongs exclusively to this general class. As for the chambers hollowed out of the marl, all of these contained pottery only of this same kind. Let us consider the caves furthest from the Khirbeh to north and south respectively, from which this type of ceramic material was recovered. Since the exploration of the cliffs was extended beyond them in either direction, they may be taken to define the geographical limits of the occupation. Moreover, the caves in the cliffs taken together with those of the marl terrace come to a combined total of more than thirty caves extending over an area of several square kilometres (Pl. XL), all of which were in use at the same period. This period coincides exactly with Periods I*b* and II of Khirbet Qumran, as is proved from the fact that the ceramic types are identical (Pl. XLII). In some cases forms characteristic of both periods have been found in the same cave, and no cave can be positively stated to have been used only during Period I*b*. The forms most frequently occurring, and in many instances the only ones attested, are the cylindrical jars, the lids, and the bowls, and these are, in fact, common to both periods. The greater part of the materials which have survived probably belongs to Period II. The absolute dates are supplied by the excavation of the Khirbeh, and here Period I*b* extends from the last third of the second century B.C. to A.D. 31, while Period II extends from the last few years before the Christian era to A.D. 68.

The use of the caves is not merely contemporaneous with Khirbet Qumran; it is organically connected with its history. The fact that it begins and ends at the same points in time as the communal occupation of the Khirbeh is significant in itself. But more than this, Khirbet Qumran lies at the centre of the area throughout which the caves are scattered, while the caves in the cliffs are grouped most closely in the vicinity of Khirbet Qumran, and none of the caves in the terrace lies more than a hundred metres from the ruins. The pottery from the caves is identical with that of the Khirbeh. The same pastes have been used and the same forms recur here, particularly in the case of the many cylindrical jars, which, apart from a single exception,[1] are not

---

[1] In a tomb at Quailba, near the site of ancient Abila in northern Transjordania, F. S. Ma'ayeh, *Annual of the Department of Antiquities of Jordan*, IV–V

found outside the area of Qumran. The indications are, therefore, that all the ceramic material was manufactured in the same
place, the workshop which was in use at Khirbet Qumran
during Periods I*b* and II.[1]

At the stage when only the first cave with manuscripts had
been discovered, and Khirbet Qumran had not yet been excavated, E. L. Sukenik put forward the hypothesis that this cave
was a *genizah*, a place, that is, where the Jews 'hid' such manuscripts as were defective, as well as books not admitted into the
Palestinian canon, heterodox works, and also secular documents
in which certain religious rules had been contravened.[2]

The same theory has also been defended by H. Del Medico,[3]
even after the excavations of Khirbet Qumran, the discovery of
eleven caves containing both manuscripts and pottery, and the
finding of some twenty further caves in which not a single fragment of writing was preserved, though they did yield examples
of the same pottery as that of the caves with manuscripts and of
Khirbet Qumran itself. We have seen the significance of the fact
that the caves were grouped around Khirbet Qumran, and the
further fact that the ceramic material found in them was identical with that of Khirbet Qumran itself. Yet in defiance of this
evidence Del Medico denies that there was any connection
between the caves and the ruins, and finds it possible to believe
that even this restricted area could have contained some thirty
genizôt, to which the following items would have been conveyed
(from sources unknown): discarded manuscripts, the lamps
which would have been kept burning before the cupboards

(1960), 116, or *Revue biblique*, LXVII (1960), 229. It is rash to conclude from
this, as P. Lapp does, that after the destruction of A.D. 68 Abila became a
place of refuge for the inhabitants of Qumran, cf. his *Palestinian Ceramic
Chronology 200 B.C.–A.D. 70* (1961), 229 and n. 53. It is noteworthy that no
jar of this type has been recorded at Masada, where so many examples have
been found of the pottery of the first century A.D., and where some refugees
from Qumran were given shelter.

[1] Cf. pp. 15–17 and 28.

[2] E. L. Sukenik, *Megillôt genuzôt*, I (1948), 16; II (1950), 20–1; *The Dead Sea
Scrolls of the Hebrew University* (1955), 22–4.

[3] H. Del Medico, 'L'état des manuscrits de Qumran I', *Vetus Testamentum*,
VII (1957), 127–38; *L'énigme des manuscrits de la Mer Morte* (1957), *passim*,
chiefly 23–31. A critical evaluation of this work appeared in *Revue biblique*,
LXVI (1959), 92–4.

where the sacred books were stored in the synagogues, the vases of foodstuffs kept locked in these same store-cupboards, and the fruit-stones from them which had been gnawed by mice. G. R. Driver likewise maintains that the caves are indeed *genizôt*. He sees the use to which they were put as reflecting a hardening of orthodox attitudes which would have taken place after the First Revolt, or alternatively, perhaps, the precarious position in which some communities found themselves, and in which, under threat of dissolution, they sought to find safe hiding-places for the compromising literature belonging to them.[1]

While these theories cannot seriously be upheld, a question which still remains to be determined is the connection between the way in which the caves were used and the buildings. We have said that most of the buildings were used for community activities. They comprise assembly-rooms, workshops, and store-rooms, but include very few rooms which would have been suitable as living quarters. To one side of them extends the great cemetery comprising more than a thousand tombs which are contemporaneous with the occupation of the buildings and the utilization of the caves.[2] There is a manifest disproportion between the number of the tombs and the number of inhabitants for whom there was room in the buildings. It is justifiable to conclude that the buildings were designed to house the central services and to provide lodgings for the administrators and guardians of the group, but that the majority of its members had their living quarters outside.

The question arises, therefore, of whether the caves were used for this purpose, but not all of them are equally suitable for habitation. All the chambers hollowed out in the marl terrace give the impression of having been designed as dwelling-places, and the objects found in them, vases for domestic use, date-stones, scraps of leather, rags, ropes, and a mat, prove that they were in fact inhabited. The natural cavities in the rock cliffs, on the other hand, vary greatly in character. There are caves with wide mouths and high roofs which still serve, on occasion, as shelters for shepherds and their flocks, as well as others which

[1] G. R. Driver, *The Judaean Scrolls* (1965), 386–91; 'Myths of Qumran', *The Annual of Leeds University Oriental Society*, vi, 1966–1968 (1969), 28.
[2] Cf. pp. 45–8.

would once have been habitable although they have subsequently been damaged by falls of rock. Caves 3Q and 11Q are cases in point. Other caves, though relatively extensive, are either so low, so narrow, or so uneven that it is doubtful whether they were ever used as dwelling-places. This applies particularly to the first two of the caves in which manuscripts were found. As for the rest of the natural fissures—and they constitute the majority of those examined—it seems quite impossible that these could ever have served as habitations. They are either very small caves, such as Cave 6Q, or crevices, or mere depressions in the rock formation.

However, the same general types of pottery were found in all three kinds of cave: those which are habitable, those which are only just so, and those which are quite uninhabitable. In all three kinds the forms which occur most frequently are jars and their lids. But in addition there are vases for everyday domestic use as well as pots, jugs, juglets, and lamps. From this it can be concluded that some members of the group would have lived in the chambers hollowed out in the marl or the more commodious of the caves in the cliffs, while others, by contrast, would have lived in huts or tents nearby. The natural cavities in the rock could have served as store-places for their provisions, and were also used as hiding-places for some of their domestic chattels when they came to abandon the area following upon the ruin of Khirbet Qumran. This is no mere hypothesis. Five wooden posts, two of them forked at the end, were found hidden in a crevice, together with fragments from four jars, several bowls, a lid, a pot, a juglet, and a lamp. These were the supporting posts of a hut or tent together with the entire household equipment it had contained.[1]

V. THE SECONDARY CEMETERIES

The members of the community, with their dwelling-places scattered throughout the area surrounding Khirbet Qumran and along the cliffs, had a large communal cemetery which had been laid out near the buildings.[2] However not all of them were

[1] Cave 17 in Discoveries in the Judaean Desert, III, 9 and pl. vii, 3.
[2] Cf. pp. 45–8.

buried there. We have actually identified two secondary cemeteries, and there may be others as well. One of the two identified
is situated on the plateau a little to the north of Khirbet Qumran. It comprises a dozen tombs grouped together, with some
others nearby. They are similar to those in the main cemetery.
Two of them were excavated in 1955. One of the skeletons they
contained was male, the other female.[1] The second cemetery was
discovered immediately to the south of Wadi Qumran, at the
foot of the marl terrace. It comprises some thirty tombs with
varying orientations. Four tombs were opened in 1956. In one
a woman was buried and the three others contained children of
between six and ten years old.[2]

VI. ARCHAEOLOGICAL REMAINS BETWEEN KHIRBET QUMRAN AND 'AIN FESHKHA

The second cemetery was discovered during the campaign of
1956, in the course of a study of the archaeological remains in
the littoral plain lying between Khirbet Qumran and the spring
of 'Ain Feshkha. At a point less than one kilometre to the south
of the Khirbeh it was just possible to discern the outlines of a
building which we located by looking down upon it as if from
an aeroplane, but actually from the heights of the cliffs overhanging it.[3] It was quadrilateral in shape, and measured about
60 × 64 m. The interior of the enclosure thus formed was empty
except for what appeared to be two rooms situated at the north-
east and south-east corners respectively, and, more certainly, a
row of rooms against the western wall. We excavated four of
these rooms. Only one or two courses of brick had survived from
the walls. The archaeological stratum is very shallow, and very
few objects were discovered. Some sherds of the type known from
Qumran were collected on the surface, but these must be set
aside since all objects which were in actual contact with the
ancient floor levels are clearly Israelite. The plan is a larger and
simpler version of that of the Israelite building at Khirbet
Qumran.[4] The ceramic material seems to be a little earlier, and
a plate covered with continuous wheel burnish may be as early

---

[1] *Revue biblique*, LXIII (1956), 569.   [2] *Ibid.*, 571.
[3] *Ibid.*, 575.   [4] See above pp. 1-2.

as the ninth century B.C. In view of the proximity of these two installations to one another it is unlikely that they were both in use at the same time. Probably the building in the plain was built first and occupied only for a short time before being replaced by the building the remains of which can be discerned beneath the ruins of Khirbet Qumran.

On the eastern side of the building in the plain is the beginning of a long wall, the remains of which can intermittently be traced following an irregular course down the sloping ground to the south (Pl. xxxa) over a distance of more than 500 m.[1] It is about one metre broad, and has been built simply on the natural gravel which lies only just beneath the actual surface of the ground. Its foundations consist of a layer of boulders followed by a layer of large stones, generally set on edge. The whole structure is hardly more than one metre high, and could never have been much higher at any stage. Bounding an area which is irrigated by small springs, it constitutes the containing wall for the plantations extending between it and the shore. Although no object has been found by which its date could be determined, in effect only two possible periods can be in question in deciding when the area was occupied. The wall was probably built during the Israelite period and at the same time as the neighbouring building (or that on the plateau of Khirbet Qumran). Its construction resembles Israelite building work in four nearby areas: the dykes or containing walls associated with the Israelite installations from the Dead Sea shore to the south of Qumran,[2] the settlements in the Buqei'a, those above the cliffs of Qumran,[3] and certain installations in the Negeb belonging to the same period.[4] The wall with which we are at present concerned, however, certainly continued in use during the period when the community was living at Khirbet Qumran, and it was probably at this time that it was extended southwards as far as 'Ain Feshkha. Here it

---

[1] *Ibid.*, 575.

[2] A wall has been discerned running parallel to the shore over a distance of more than 600 m. between 'Ain Ghuweir and 'Ain Turaba, I. Blake, *Revue biblique*, LXXIII (1966), 565; P. Bar-Adon, *ibid.*, LXXVII (1970), 399.

[3] F. M. Cross and J. T. Milik, 'Explorations in the Judaean Buqê'ah', *Bulletin of the American Schools of Oriental Research*, **142** (April 1956), 8–9.

[4] M. Evenari, *et al.*, 'The Ancient Desert Agriculture of the Negeb', *Israel Exploration Journal*, VIII (1958), 239–47.

reappears, still continuing in the same direction, as a wall of different construction and having connection with the buildings about to be described. It is impossible to accept L. M. Pákozdy's interpretation to the effect that this wall would have supported a conduit distributing water from 'Ain Feshkha through the gardens.[1] There is no vestige of archaeological evidence for this, and it is ruled out by the level of the wall relative to the spring.

Near this ancient wall, and about halfway along the part that is visible, we excavated a small square structure (Pl. xxxb) of about 12 × 12 m.[2] It has a door facing eastwards, and the inside is divided into three rooms. Platforms of masonry were built into the north-eastern and south-eastern corners. The walls are of good construction, though only one or two courses of them have survived. The pottery, though scarce and much fragmented, is contemporaneous with that of the Khirbeh. Only one coin has been recovered, and it is illegible. This small building probably has some connection with one or other of the periods of community life at Khirbet Qumran, having been a watch-tower or a functional building relating to the agricultural work practised within the circumference of the long wall.

The littoral plain extending southwards from this building (Pl. xli) is irrigated by numerous small springs. Today the slightly brackish water from these nourishes reeds, brushwood, and tamarisks, forming a broad patch of green in the desert landscape. Still further to the south the more plentiful spring of 'Ain Feshkha and the small springs near it are surrounded by another patch of green. Between the square building and the area about 'Ain Feshkha no visible signs are to be found of any ancient buildings except some masonry work round one of the springs which, to judge from the carving of the stones, appears to be Byzantine.

VII. FESHKHA

Just to the north of the spring of Feshkha, however, lies a more important installation. Its presence was recognized in 1956 from

---

[1] L. M. Pákozdy, 'Der wirtschaftliche Hintergrund der Gemeinschaft von Qumran', Qumran-Probleme. Vorträge des Leipziger Symposions über Qumran-Probleme vom 9. bis 14. Oktober 1961 (1963), 276–9.

[2] Revue biblique, LXIII (1956), 576.

the few stones which were visible on the surface, for in recent times it had become completely silted over. It was excavated in 1958 (Pl. xxxiia). It consists of a fairly large building, flanked on the south by an enclosure with a lean-to shed and on the north by a courtyard equipped with basins.[1]

1. *The Building* (Pls. xxxiib and xli)

The building forms a rectangular whole of 24 × 18 m. The entrance is from the east, consisting of two doors built in well-dressed stone. One in the centre of the outer wall opens on to a porch (loc. 11 A), from which a broad opening gives access to the inner courtyard, loc. 4. The other door, immediately to the north of the first, opens on to a paved passage, loc. 9 (Pl. xxxiiia), which in ancient times led to the room at 11 A and the long room at 21–2. It is hardly possible to explain why these two doors should have been placed so close to one another except by presuming that the western end of the passage was originally closed so that it did not lead into the inner courtyard, since the central door already gave access to this. It can also be concluded that one of the entrances was designed for human use and the other for animals.

The inner courtyard is surrounded by structures on all four sides. On the eastern side, apart from the two entrances, two buildings are situated in the northern and southern corners respectively. The first of these is one end of a store-room, 21–2, which we are about to describe more fully. The second, situated in the southern corner, is 11 B, a room with a drain running diagonally across it and carrying off the water from the courtyard to the outside of the building. It is impossible to determine the purpose of this room. All that can be noted is that 32 small coins were recovered from it, a larger number than was found in any other locus in the ruins. The two main rooms seem to have been those to the west, locs. 3 and 5. They have fine rabbeted doorways. Room 3 has a paved floor and two recessed cupboards in its eastern wall, while Room 5 has a recessed cupboard and a semicircular area of flagstones against the east wall. A fair quantity of pottery and a number of coins were found.

[1] *Revue biblique*, LXVI (1959), 225–55.

The whole of the north wing was taken up by a long room with a single doorway giving access to the paved passage (Pl. xxxiii*b*). Locs. 21, 22, and 22 *bis*, are divided from one another simply by low narrow walls, bench-like structures serving as divisions. Though a fairly large quantity of pottery was found here, it was very badly fragmented. The room was most probably a store-room. Built against this long room, and in the north-west corner of the courtyard, was a small room, loc. 6. Opening on to the southern side of the courtyard were two paved rooms divided by a wall of poor construction, which may be secondary, locs. 7 and 10. These too may have been store-rooms.

A staircase situated in the south-east corner leads up to a terrace lying above the rooms on the south side and, as will be shown, extending over the large room on the north side. The rooms on the west were surmounted by an upper storey. This has been established from the number of stones found fallen outside the building and in locs. 3 and 5, though despite this the walls here have been preserved to a height of two metres; in fact, in the course of excavating these rooms the debris from two ceilings was discovered, with an intervening layer containing sherds. The fact that locs. 3 and 5 had an upper storey consisting of more than one room accounts for a further feature, namely the large column standing in the western part of the courtyard, one metre of which has survived. It served to support a gangway between the two terraces in the north and south wings. The single stairway in the corner of the courtyard led up to this gangway, and at the same time it gave access to the rooms built over locs. 3 and 5.

It may be conjectured that the rooms found on the western side, both at ground level and on the upper storey, and perhaps also the room in the south-east corner at 11 B, were designed as living quarters or offices, the rest of the building being given over to store-rooms. Clearly it is not a private dwelling, and is more suitable for the requirements of a community.

The description we have just given applies to the building in its best preserved state, and the one for which the archaeological evidence is most plentiful. But there was an earlier stage in its existence. In the room in the corner of the courtyard, loc. 6, two distinct levels can clearly be discerned; there are two floors with two door-sills, one above the other. Again in the long room in the north wing we find two levels, for here also two floors can be distinguished, while the small dividing wall between locs. 22 and 22 *bis* was built above a jar which had been buried during the first period. The pavement of the passage at 9 had been renewed. The staircase leading to the terraces is a later addition, since it blocks up an earlier doorway. At the earlier stage there was no staircase, and therefore no gangway across the courtyard either, nor any upper rooms on the western side. Thus the two periods can be distinguished from the secondary modifications to the building, and there was probably an intervening period of abandonment. In fact outside the north wall, and especially opposite locs. 5 and 21, piles of rubbish and broken pottery were discovered containing the same types of sherds as those found in the lower level of locs. 21 and 22. This constitutes the rubble cleared out of the building at the time when it came to be occupied afresh. There is nothing to indicate that the first period was brought to an end by any violent destruction. In contrast the second period ended with a fire, the traces of which are especially apparent in the long room on the north side, and from the fact that throughout the entire building ceilings and walls have fallen in.

Yet a third period must be distinguished, in which parts of the ruins were reoccupied. This affected only the north wing of the building (Pl. xxxv*a*). Loc. 22 *bis* was abandoned—doubtless because it had become too blocked up by the collapse of the north-east corner—and on top of the low dividing wall between locs. 22 and 22 *bis* a wall was built to hold back the rubble. Only the west face of this wall was dressed. A further wall on the west served to hold back the rubble of loc. 21 and part of loc. 22. By levelling this rubble a large room was constructed on the western side, giving access to a lower chamber which took up almost the whole of the earlier loc. 22 (this is loc. 15, Pl. xxxv*a*). The communicating door between this locus (and also locs. 21 and 22 *bis*) and the passage at 9 was blocked up, and a new doorway was pierced in the same wall at the level of the flattened out rubble just to the west of the low wall which had formerly divided loc. 22 from 21. Since the threshold of this doorway was 1·50 m. higher than the floor-levels of the preceding period, a

platform of large stones was built on the outside, sloping down
towards the pavement of the passage at 9. Access to the structure
as a whole was through the doorway in the eastern façade, which
had formerly led into this passage. To the south of the passage
the rubble in loc. 11 A and the corner of the courtyard was contained by blocking up the doorway between 11 A and 9, and
also by means of a wall of poor construction running westwards
from this point. The remainder of the building seems not to have
been re-utilized.

A careful study of the walls and floors, therefore, enables us to
distinguish three periods, and the pottery and coins provide
material for assigning them dates. Unfortunately moist earth
impregnated with salt has penetrated into the ruins, defacing the
pottery and causing extreme oxidization of the coins. In spite
of this, sufficient pottery forms have survived, and sufficient
coins have remained legible, to enable us to put forward the
conclusions which follow.

The main period of occupation, and that which has been
described at greatest length, is Period II, and for this there is no
room for doubt; it is contemporaneous with Period II of Khirbet
Qumran. It is true that there is a scarcity of jars, and that none
of the cylindrical jars of Khirbet Qumran and the caves has been
found here. But among the smaller vessels all the forms characteristic of the class are to be found: spherical juglets, ampullae,
'Herodian' lamps, plates with moulded rims, assymetrical flasks,
and wide-mouthed pots (Pls. xxxivb and xlii). The parallelism
here has been confirmed and given an added precision from
the evidence of the coins. The earliest examples belonging to
Period II are four coins of Herod Archelaus, and next in order
come 32 coins of the Procurators and 45 of Agrippa I. A single
coin of Tyre of A.D. 36/37 should also be included in this group.
The latest in the series is a coin of the second year of the First
Revolt, struck in A.D. 67/68. Thus Period II of 'Ain Feshkha
corresponds perfectly to Period II of Khirbet Qumran. The
periods during which the two installations were respectively in
use both fall within the same chronological limits.

Apart from the pottery and the coins, one of the most interesting objects found at this level is a large vase of soft limestone,
0·70 m. high, which we were able to reconstruct from a great

number of fragments (Pl. xxxiva). It was found shattered in the corner of loc. 21, where it had fallen from the terrace at the time when the building was destroyed. Isolated fragments of similar vases have been recovered at Khirbet Qumran in almost every season of digging, and many others have already been found in the excavations of the Ophel at Jerusalem. They have been assigned to the Herodian period, but no complete example was known before that from Feshkha.[1] On the upper part of the vase is an engraved border of 4×5 cm. enclosing two lines in semi-cursive Hebrew. Unfortunately the letters have been only very lightly inscribed, and are almost indistinguishable. The first line probably reads: בשנת אחת, 'in the first year', but the second line, half of which is missing due to a break, still defies decipherment.

For the earlier occupation, that of Period I, far less evidence is available. So far as the inside of the building is concerned, all that can be attributed to it with any certainty are the following: a jar buried in the lower of the two floors of loc. 6, some sherds from the same stratum, several jars sunk into the lower floor of locs. 21 and 22, but sheared off below the neck, which is the distinguishing feature, some beakers, bowls, and plates, a lid, and a great quantity of sherds. On the outside of the north wall, however, there were piles of rubbish and broken vases which had been thrown there when the building was cleared out at the beginning of Period II. They belong, therefore, to Period I. It has been possible to reconstruct some of the forms, and, like the pottery and sherds from the lower stratum of locs. 21 and 22, they have their exact counterparts in Period I*b* of Khirbet Qumran, especially for the forms which are absent from the pottery of Period II of Khirbet Qumran and Feshkha: flat plates (or lids) with chamfered rims, flared beakers with thin walls, and the reinforced necks of large jars (Pl. xlii).

Very few legible coins can be attributed to this period, but

[1] R. A. S. Macalister and J. G. Duncan, *Excavations on the Hill of Ophel, Jerusalem*, Palestine Exploration Fund Annual, iv (1926), 147–50. By means of a copious use of plaster one such vase had been reconstructed from some of the fragments at the Palestine Archaeological Museum, *Gallery Book, Persian, Hellenistic, Roman, Byzantine Periods* (1943), no. 1092. Another complete vase has emerged from the recent excavations of the Jewish Quarter at Jerusalem, N. Avigad, *Israel Exploration Journal*, xx (1970), 6 and pl. 4: B.

those that can are interesting. A bronze coin of Ptolemy II
(247–245 B.C.), recovered from the lower threshold of loc. 6,[1]
must be considered an anomaly. It is at least one and a half
centuries earlier than the other coins, and is not associated with
any ceramic material of its own period. It must be concluded
that this is a chance instance of a bronze piece having been kept
over a long period for the value of its metal, and this one isolated
piece cannot be used as evidence for determining the date at
which Feshkha was first occupied. But there are four coins of
Alexander Jannaeus, one of which derives from the lowest
stratum of loc. 21, and one coin of Antigonus Mattathias discovered together with a coin of one of the Hasmoneans (which
one is uncertain) on the lower floor of loc. 6. Finally a coin of
Herod, dated in the third year of his reign, has been recovered
from loc. 5, immediately above the level of the natural soil. It
provides important evidence for determining the date when
Period I ended. These coins of the third year of Herod were
struck in 37 B.C., the beginning of Herod's effective rule, following upon his victory over Antigonus, but three years after his
coronation by the senate in 40 B.C.[2] On this showing the end of
Period I falls after 37 B.C. Unfortunately in this particular room
there is no very clear distinction between the two levels of
occupation, and the ascription of this coin to Period I is only
probable. The fact remains that the coins which can be ascribed
with certainty to Alexander Jannaeus and Antigonus Mattathias,
as well as the entire ceramic material, do establish that Period I
of Feshkha corresponds to Period I*b* of Khirbet Qumran.

Period III, the final period of occupation, is more difficult to
date. This was a time when a comparatively small part of the

---

[1] Described in *Revue biblique*, LXVI (1959), 249. This type is attributed to
Ptolemy II by J. N. Svoronos, Τὰ Νομίσματα τοῦ Κράτους τῶν Πτολεμαίων,
1904–8, no. 708 and pl. xx. 18. Identical coins have been discovered at
Beth-Sur, O. R. Sellers, *The Citadel of Beth-Zur* (1933), 77, nos. 23 f., at the
same time as numerous other coins of the Ptolemies, and associated with a
type of pottery different from that of Feshkha.

[2] B. Kanael, 'The Coins of King Herod of the Third Year', *Jewish
Quarterly Review*, XLII (1951–2), 261–4. According to U. Rapaport these coins
were struck in 37 B.C., but prior to the occupation of Jerusalem by Herod,
cf. his article, 'Note sur la chronologie des monnaies hérodiennes', *Revue
numismatique*, VIᵉ Série, x (1968), 64–75. For our purposes, however, this point
is of secondary importance.

ruins was re-utilized, namely locs. 21 and 22. The very small amount of pottery yielded by this upper level is indistinguishable from the pottery of Period II. The coins are few: one coin struck at Antioch during Domitian's reign, A.D. 81–96, was found on the threshold of the new doorway which was pierced above loc. 21. A hoard of eighteen bronze coins, stuck together by oxidization, was found lying on the top of the retaining wall built to the east of this locus, and the imprint of the bag in which they had been kept was preserved in the encrustation of the oxide (Pl. xxxvc). This hoard consists of seventeen coins of Agrippa II ranging in date from A.D. 78 to 95, and a bronze coin, much defaced, bearing two countermarks which have not been identified. Three coins from the Second Revolt of A.D. 132–5 were found above loc. 21. Finally a very worn coin of Aelia Capitolina from the reign of Antoninus Pius, A.D. 138–61, had slid down between the stones of the wall on the top of which the coins of Agrippa II were found. It is an isolated example which must have been lost by a passer-by.

A further object was discovered fairly near the top of the pile of debris filling loc. 10. It is a weight of white limestone in the shape of a bulging cylinder (Pl. xxxvb), and in the first edition of this book (pp. 54–5) I assigned it to Period III. On one of its faces it bears the three letters LEB very clearly incised. The form of the letters is characteristic of the first century A.D. I tentatively suggested that they should be read as a poor attempt at writing the letters LIB, an abbreviation of *libra* used in Latin inscriptions. This weight weighs 729 gr., which corresponds almost exactly to the Phoenician mina (with its theoretical weight of 727·5 gr.), as used in Palestine. Now the Talmud states that the pound is equivalent in weight to the mina.[1] In translating Dioscorides Pliny renders μνᾶ by *libra*, and the experts in metrication conclude that μνᾶ should be equated with λίτρα, or *mina* (*mna*) with *libra*. As one of them tersely states, *mna libra Graeciae*.[2] The difficulty is that Josephus contradicts the Talmud by explicitly asserting that the Jewish mina equals two and a half pounds,[3] while the equivalence established by the Greek and

---

[1] S. Krauss, *Talmudische Archäologie*, II (1911), 403.
[2] References in *Thesaurus Linguae Graecae*, s.v. μνᾶ and λίτρα; *Thesaurus Linguae Latinae*, s.v. *mina*. [3] *Ant.*, XIV, vii, 106.

Latin authors cannot be justified as it stands except as applied
to the Attic mina and the Roman pound. Now the Attic mina
weighed 436 gr., which is nowhere near the weight of the
Feshkha piece. It is possible to find a better explanation.[1] The
object found at Feshkha belongs to the class of weights which
have dates inscribed on them. The first 'L' is the symbol of the
'year', known to Greek epigraphists. The 'E' has the numerical
value of five. The final letter, 'B', could also have a numerical
value, namely 2, and could serve to indicate that the weight is
equivalent to two light minas of about 360 gr., a unit known to
have been in use. A slightly different explanation has been
suggested by certain recent discoveries. A weight of three (Attic)
minas bears the inscription L ΛB BAC HP . . ., 'Year 32 of King
Herod (the Great) . . .'.[2] In a recent article B. Mazar describes six
inscribed weights discovered in the course of his excavations near
the wall of the Jerusalem temple.[3] One of these weights (365 gr.)
bears the inscription, LE BACI/ΛEΩC/AΦP MNA, which Mazar
reads as 'Year 5 of King A(ΓPIΠΠA) Φ(IΛOKAICA)P, one
mina'. The title which, according to this theory, has been
abridged in this manner also appears on the coins of Agrippa I,
and the weight is equivalent to that of the light mina. Another
weight (735·5 gr.) is inscribed 'LE BACI ΛEΩC'. Three weights
are marked with the date alone, ΓE. They weigh 372·8 gr.,
85·2 gr., and 643·6 gr. respectively, but the last-mentioned has
been chipped. Finally a large weight of 2706·5 gr. is inscribed
'LEA', and the third letter here could stand for 'Agrippa'. In
fact Mazar assigns all these weights to Agrippa I's reign, the
fifth year of which corresponds to A.D. 41/42. If we take these as
a basis for comparison, we might conclude that the B on the
Feshkha weight could be an abbreviation of BACIΛEΩC. Such
an abbreviation is, however, without precedent elsewhere. A
further point that calls for explanation is why these official
weights should differ so much among themselves, even though

[1] I am indebted to Mr. Arye Ben-David of Jerusalem, to whom I owe the
explanation which follows.

[2] Y. Meshorer, 'A Stone Weight from the Reign of Herod', *Israel Exploration Journal*, xx (1970), 97–8.

[3] B. Mazar, *The Archaeological Excavations near the Mount of the Temple.
Second Report* (in Hebrew) (1971), 19 and pl. 26.

they were made under the same king and during the same year. The question remains open.

The nature of the two phases of occupation is fairly clear. They are exactly contemporaneous with Periods I*b* and II of Khirbet Qumran. The installations at Feshkha are close to those at Khirbet Qumran; the architecture is similar; the ceramic material is homogeneous. All these signs point to the fact that the two were organically connected. They were inhabited by the same community, and it is this that explains their common history. At Khirbet Qumran we have distinguished an additional phase, Period I*a*, but this was brief and relatively unimportant.[1] There are no points of connection between it and Feshkha, but this is easily explained on the supposition that the occupation of Feshkha began only when the developing community built the large complex at Khirbet Qumran belonging to Period I*b*. This marks the point at which the community established itself in the area definitively.

The end of Period I*b* at Khirbet Qumran was marked by a fire and an earthquake, and for a time, between Periods I*b* and II, the settlement was abandoned. At Feshkha the situation is less clear, but the fact that the building was cleared out, accounting for the piles of rubbish against the north wall, suggests that this too was abandoned for a time between Periods I and II. On the other hand there are no traces of a fire or earthquake having occurred. The explanation may be that the earthquake which shook the buildings at Khirbet Qumran was not felt three kilometres away at Feshkha, in an area which has a different geological formation. But if Feshkha was a dependency belonging to the same community as Khirbet Qumran it would have been natural for this secondary establishment to have been abandoned at the same time as the main centre.

Some authors have sought to draw a distinction between the two events at Khirbet Qumran: first, the fire, which would have been kindled by enemies, and would have occasioned the ruin and abandonment of the site before the effective reign of Herod the Great began in 37 B.C., and second the earthquake in 31 B.C., when the buildings which it affected would already have been empty. We have thought it more probable that the fire and the

[1] Cf. p. 3.

abandonment were consequences arising from the earthquake.[1] Evidence in support of this view can be adduced from the history of Feshkha. If Khirbet Qumran was indeed destroyed by enemies, then it would be astonishing for them to have spared the dependent settlement of Feshkha. Yet at Feshkha there was neither a fire nor any destruction at the end of Period I. On the other hand if the coin referred to above, from the third year of Herod's reign, does indeed belong to Period I, it is evidence of the fact that Feshkha was still being occupied in 37 B.C., at a time when, on the alternative hypothesis, Khirbet Qumran would already have been abandoned.

In contrast to Period I, Period II is brought to an end by a violent destruction affecting both sites. The latest coins are: at Khirbet Qumran, several coins from the third year of the First Revolt; at Feshkha, where the numismatic evidence is much more scanty, one coin from the second year of the First Revolt. It must be concluded that both establishments were destroyed at the same point in time and by the same adversaries. Feshkha too fell in June A.D. 68 at the hands of the Roman soldiers, and this episode put an end to community life throughout the whole area of Qumran.

It is more difficult to determine the course of events during Period III at Feshkha. As we have seen, at Khirbet Qumran an outpost of Roman soldiers seems to have been installed in the ruins, remaining there for some years. Then, after it had been abandoned for some sixty years, the insurgents of the Second Revolt took refuge there. It might be tempting to look for a parallel development at Feshkha, and in fact there is one further point of convergence between the history of the two sites: the presence of three coins in the ruins of Feshkha shows that they too were put to use during the Second Revolt. Yet whereas at Khirbet Qumran a well-defined group of coins was found, ranging in date from A.D. 67/68 to A.D. 72/73, and only a single isolated coin of Agrippa II, at Feshkha there is a hoard of seventeen coins of Agrippa II, as well as one coin of Domitian and one stray coin of Antoninus Pius. Thus there are discrepancies in the numismatic evidence, and it appears that Feshkha remained abandoned for some little time after the destruction

[1] Cf. pp. 20–21.

of Period II.[1] It is unlikely that the presence of the coin of Domitian and the small hoard of coins of Agrippa II can be explained by supposing that after A.D. 73 the military post at Khirbet Qumran was transferred to Feshkha, and it is more reasonable to accept that Roman soldiers were never stationed at Feshkha.

The coins of Domitian and Agrippa II may perhaps indicate that Feshkha was occupied to some small extent by an independent group at the end of the first century A.D., but we cannot altogether exclude the possibility that the coins were brought there by the rebels of A.D. 132-5, who left some of their own coins behind.[2] On the first hypothesis these unknown occupiers of the reign of Agrippa II would have been responsible for the extremely cursory modifications introduced to the north wing of the ruined building. On the second hypothesis these poorly constructed works should be attributed to the Jewish rebels. This is a secondary question, and the significant point is that the two main periods of Feshkha, Periods I and II are parallel to two important periods in the life of the community at Khirbet Qumran, and also that throughout the whole of this time the two sites were connected. The part which Feshkha played in this community life as a whole will be clarified when we come to study certain installations associated with the building.

2. *The Enclosure to the South*

To the south-west of the building there lies an enclosure, the walls of which, or such parts of them as can be recognized, describe a square of about 40 m. on each side. Formerly, however, the enclosure extended further east, though on this side the boundary wall has disappeared. The north wall was once attached to the south-west corner of the building, but the

[1] Here I am correcting the conclusions which I tentatively put forward in *Revue biblique*, LXVI (1959), 251-3. I now feel that these conclusions are decisively contradicted by the numismatic evidence.

[2] There is no difference between the level at which the coins of Domitian and Agrippa II were found and that from which the coins of the Second Revolt derive. In any case the positions in which they were found (cf. p. 67) indicates that they were lost at some point later than the reconstruction of Period III. This excludes the possibility that they were left through forgetfulness by passers-by in the ruins of Period II.

connecting piece is no longer there, probably because it was used to provide stones for the reconstruction of loc. 20 at the time of the Byzantine settlement of which we shall shortly have to speak.

On to this same north wall was built an extension (Pl. xxxvi) which began near the building with a square element, loc. 20, and it had a door to the east. Its walls were based directly upon a pavement which was prolonged eastwards, and also for some distance southwards. We traced this part of the pavement by means of an excavation trench. The south wall of loc. 20 has a prolongation to the west consisting of a line of rectangular supports made of masonry. It runs parallel to the containing wall to the north, and up to the containing wall on the west. The difference between these supports varies from 1·75 m. to 2·50 m., and they have survived only to a height of 0·45 m. at the most. However, it is clear that their purpose was to hold up the roof, the other edge of which rested on the containing wall. Wooden beams may have been interposed between the roof and the top of the supports. The area covered by this roof was paved with fairly small cobblestones in loc. 17 (in the western part of this the pavement has almost entirely disappeared), and by larger cobblestones in loc. 18. To correct the natural slope of the terrain towards the east the floor-level of loc. 18 was artificially raised and held in place by a parapet built at the dividing line between locs. 17 and 18. The line of supports is continued in loc. 19, which occupies the north-west corner of the enclosure, but here the floor is of beaten earth. On this floor a layer of ashes was found containing numerous sherds, whereas there were no ashes and very few sherds in locs. 17 and 18. Unfortunately the boundary between locs. 18 and 19 had been obliterated by the modern track. Although we excavated this, it had destroyed every vestige of ancient remains. It is certain that one of the masonry supports was uprooted in this way. It is not impossible that there was once a wall closing loc. 19 to the east.

The installation as a whole gives the impression of being secondary. It has already been pointed out that the walls of loc. 20 were based on a pavement which continued beyond and outside it. To provide a bed for the first masonry supports leading from this room to the west, a pavement of small stones was inserted, which has the appearance of being contempora-

neous with the containing wall, and which is extended southwards beyond the supports. The raised pavement superimposed
on loc. 18 is of a different kind, and the supports associated with
it seem to have been built at the same time as itself. Most of this
long building, which was open at the side to a width of nearly
30 m., was not used for living quarters. Only the two ends could
have had this function, loc. 20, which is enclosed, and loc. 19,
which may have been so and in which some domestic pottery
was found. Possibly this building may have served as a tempo-
rary shelter for men or animals. But one peculiarity must be
noticed: the supports of loc. 17 are linked by a line of small
stones which are higher than the level of the inside pavement,
but gradually slope down on the outside towards the pavement
there until they are flush with it. This was a way of ensuring that
the drainage water did not penetrate into the covered space.
The structure seems, therefore, to be a shelter, a sort of lean-to
shed, serving either to dry off, or to preserve in a state of dryness,
some unidentified product. In Europe one might think of a barn
for hay or straw, but no examples of barns of this kind have been
found among the antiquities of Palestine, and the region of
Qumran and Feshkha is far from being suitable for the growing
of grass- or corn-crops. Reeds grow abundantly and must have
been turned to good account for basket-making, as they still are
to this day, but nowadays the reeds are simply collected into
little piles to dry, with stones placed on top of them.

One possible hypothesis is that this shed was a drying-house
for dates, or rather where the dates, having been picked before
they were fully ripe, were spread out to ripen off. It is true that
the normal practice is to expose them to the sun. But Jordanians
who are expert in the cultivation of dates have seen the installation at Feshkha, and are convinced that it could have been used
for this purpose. They assure me that dates for domestic con-
sumption are better to eat and keep better when ripened in the
shade. This fits the only large-scale cultivation which seems
possible in this area. The date-palm likes slightly salt water, and
lives with its roots in the water and its branches in the sun; it
requires a high temperature during the summer in order to
bring its fruit to maturity. These conditions are fulfilled in the
tract of land extending from Feshkha to Khirbet Qumran.

Besides the main springs of 'Ain Feshkha and 'Ain el-Ghazal there are a number of lesser springs, all slightly brackish. The roots of the trees could very soon reach the level of the water, which is close to the surface throughout. The beams of palm-wood, palm-leaves, and dates discovered in the ruins of Khirbet Qumran and the caves show that palms were formerly cultivated nearby. An installation connected with this form of cultivation would not be out of place at Feshkha, but this shed could have had many other uses, and the question must remain open.

The walls on the west and south of the enclosure have been cleared on both sides, and do not show any traces of masonry attached to them, such as could have constituted the beginnings of a building or dividing wall. Nor are there any surface traces inside the enclosure indicative of a buried building. It seems, therefore, that the enclosure was empty apart from the shed built against its north wall.

This is the state of the enclosure in Period II, but there had already been a different enclosure in Period I. It was bounded on the west by a wall which extended the western wall of the building towards the south. Two courses of this wall have survived at the point at which it is attached to the south-west corner of the building, but it disappears almost immediately beneath the pavement of the enclosure of Period II. It reappears twenty metres to the south, beyond the surviving part of this same pavement. It continues at least as far as the modern track, and the southern wall of the enclosure of Period II abuts upon it. The position of the other sides of the enclosure of Period I is unknown. This enclosure was empty, apart from the shed of Period II, and lay near the spring, so that it could have served as a paddock for the livestock.

The enclosure remained unused during Period III, but much later the square room at the eastern end of the shed, loc. 20, was rebuilt (Pl. xxxvia). The walls were repaired with blocks which were probably torn out of the wall of the enclosure at the point where it was attached to the building. This would explain why the connection has disappeared. The threshold was heightened. Inside, the walls were faced with a coating of pebbles which must have been dug up from the pavement of Period II. This explains how the section of pavement between loc. 20 and the corner of the building came to be missing. The coating does not go right down to the original pavement inside the building, but rests on a layer of earth from 10 to 25 cm. in thickness. All the sherds associated with this work of restoration are Byzantine. To these may be added a lamp and juglet of the same period which were found together in a layer of silt against the north wall of the enclosure.

Light is thrown on the significance of this minor Byzantine occupation by a written document. John Moschus relates a story[1] which may be summarized as follows:

In the mountain of Marda[2] dwelt certain anchorites who also had a garden six miles away near the seashore. A man in their service lived there, and whenever they needed vegetables they used to harness an ass, which would proceed quite on its own to the gardener's house, knock on the door with its head, and return up the mountain, still on its own, loaded with provisions.

Marda being the modern Khirbet Mird, situated in the Buqei'a above Feshkha, the sea in the story is the Dead Sea, and the gardens six miles from Marda could not be situated anywhere else except near 'Ain Feshkha, from which a way leads up across the Buqei'a to Khirbet Mird, nine kilometres to the west. It is interesting that the monks of Marda cultivated a garden at 'Ain Feshkha and obtained vegetables from it. This piece of information confirms the fact that agriculture could be practised in the area in ancient times.

3. *The Enclosure to the North*

Another enclosure was built during Period II. It was attached to the north-west corner of the building, and extended 23 m. to the north and almost 40 m. to the east. The western half of this courtyard seems to have been left empty. In fact no attempt was ever made to set up any structure backing either on to the north wall of the building or on to the western and southern walls of the enclosure, the whole of which have been cleared. A trench was opened in the centre of the area running from east to west, and although it was carried down to virgin soil, the only objects found were two ancient floors separated by 25 cm. of deposit.

The eastern half, on the other hand, is taken up with a system

---

[1] John Moschus, *Pratum Spirituale, PG* lxxxvii, 3026.
[2] Following the reading of the Latin text.

of basins and small channels (Pls. xxxvii and xli). The water was led in from loc. 29 and passed through the north wall of the enclosure by way of two openings separated by a dressed stone slab (Pl. xxxviiib). The flow was directed south-eastwards down a channel opening into a rectangular tank (loc. 23) of 0·80 m. in depth. An overflow was provided by means of a short channel leading out northwards under the boundary wall, after which the water drained away down the natural slope of the ground.

Two other channels led away from the tank at 23. One was directed southwards, initially to feed a large square basin, loc. 24 (Pl. xxxviiia). The basin was a little more than one metre deep, and its floor and walls were coated with plaster, only parts of which have survived. On the bottom of the basin this plaster was covered by a white deposit, generally thinly spread, but piled up to a greater thickness in the east corner. In fact the basin slopes downwards slightly towards the east, and the mouth of a conduit leads out level with the bottom where it is at its deepest against the south-east wall. The opening of this conduit is formed by a stone with a smooth round hole carved in it so that the basin could easily be plugged or unplugged for emptying.

On the other side of the basin wall there is a prolongation of the conduit consisting of a trough cut into the paved floor of a small sunken element, and opening into a rectangular pit dug against the wall (Pl. xxxviiia). The pit is 1·30 m. deep, and one could descend into it by means of a stone projecting from one of its sides, and another stone embedded in its bottom. The pit had a coating of lime, sand, and gravel, though this has survived only in some parts. From the eastern corner a flight of three steps leads out on to the pavement surrounding the basins, and in this pavement a steeply sloping plaster-coated trough has been dug. The fact that it is certainly connected with the flight of steps shows that its function was to carry away the waste water drawn up from the pit.

The channel leading out of the tank at loc. 23, therefore, first fed the basin at loc. 24 and then curved southwards round two sides of this, terminating at a point beyond its southern corner. Here it discharged its contents down three steps into a rectangular area with a gently sloping paved floor (on which vestiges of plaster have survived), and so down to the first of two pits separated by a dividing wall. This first pit (Pl. xxxviiia) is larger and deeper than the second, to be described shortly. So much water had infiltrated that it was not possible to empty it completely, but it was established that the masonry extended downwards at least 1·55 m. below the level of the pavement at the south corner. Fragments of plaster intermingled with the damp earth filling showed that it too had been coated with plaster.

Another channel from the tank at loc. 23 takes a south-easterly course, leading directly into a rectangular basin 3·50 m. long by 8 m. broad, loc. 26. At the point where it arrives at this basin the channel is slightly raised and broadened, a deliberate device for ensuring that the water sank gently into the basin in a smooth unbroken flow. Our conclusions on this point are confirmed by the fact that a parapet runs along the inner wall of the basin a good metre below the mouth of the channel. In excavating this basin we were once more brought to a halt by the water which had infiltrated. The masonry extends downwards at least 0·75 m. below the existing water level, and there are traces of plaster.

Between the basin at loc. 24 and the channel which feeds the other at loc. 26 is an area paved with large slabs except for one point where a shallow depression had been left. Here a jar was found lying intact. To the south-east, and at a slightly lower level, there is a further pavement, a continuation of the one made of slabs, but composed of slightly smaller stones. Between the channel running along the edge of this pavement and the boundary wall lies an open space in which two floors have been discerned. Although there is a distance of 0·20 m. between them they do not represent two different stages in the history of the installation. The first is a floor of lime and is hard. The construction is contemporaneous with that of the channel and the basins. The upper floor had not been specially treated. It simply marks the point beyond which this space had not been put to any special use. On the second floor two oblong stones were found, roughly carved into the form of cylinders (Pl. xxxviib). They were certainly not intended for any building. They could not have rolled here from anywhere else. They are lying on the spot where they were left after having been put to some use which we must try to determine. A similar stone was found at the bottom of Basin 24, and another in Basin 26. Evidently they had been pushed there from the platform nearby.

These basins are certainly not cisterns for storing water. This is ruled out by their shallowness, the narrowness of the two pits adjoining Basin 24, and the complexity of the system by which they were fed. They are not baths. This is ruled out by the shape of the two pits and the absence of steps throughout. This is an industrial installation in which water played a major part.

An initial question arises, therefore: whence did the water originate? It did not come from any of the existing springs. The beginning of the system of channels, which is visible at loc. 29, is almost five metres higher than the spring of 'Ain Feshkha, and even the highest of the small springs nearby is still three metres below it. We explored the possibility that here, as at Qumran, the water might derive from intermittent torrents flowing down the nearest wadi as a result of the winter rains, and that it might have been brought to the settlement by means of an aqueduct. However, there is no trace of the major engineering works that this would necessarily have entailed, and the hypothesis must be discarded. It will be remembered, however, that since ancient times the complex of subterranean streams has altered, and it still remains a possibility that there was once a spring higher up. Now between the building and the modern track to the west there is a slight depression which seems to mark the site of just such an ancient spring. Originally the stream from it flowed southwards, and the bed which it had carved out can still be recognized under the north wall of the southern enclosure. At the centre of loc. 17 the foundations of this wall consist of a heap of large stones blocking a ditch which extended in a northerly direction. At the time when the wall was built the stream can no longer have been flowing along this ditch, because it had been diverted eastwards from the spring to feed the basins. It flowed to loc. 29 (Pl. xxxviiib), where it was caught and guided into the enclosure, and through this to the basins. At other points between Feshkha and Khirbet Qumran there are signs of several dried-up springs at a level higher than the existing ones. From all this a further important corollary may perhaps ensue. Emerging as it did at a higher level, the water from these springs did not have to traverse those lower levels which formed the littoral of the Dead Sea and so were charged to an increasing extent with various kinds of salt. Hence it was probably purer in quality and more suitable for human use. We may recall the garden at Feshkha where the monks of Marda used to cultivate vegetables.

A further problem which we would like to solve is the purpose for which the water was brought into the northern enclosure, and the nature of the industry which the basins and channels were designed to serve. I have put forward the hypothesis that it was a place for the curing of hides.[1] This kind of industry involves much washing, rinsing, and repeated steeping of the materials over a long period, and uses up large quantities of water. The dried skins are first subjected to a process designed to make them supple once more. They are steeped in water, either flowing or frequently renewed, which cleanses them and causes them to swell. The tank at 23 could have been used in this way. By plugging the exit channels to the south and east, thereby causing the overflow to function, a constant stream of running water could have been maintained.

Next comes the process of depilation, which involves stripping the hides and scraping off the hair. For this depilation process they are macerated in basins of lime-water. First they are passed through weaker baths of the solution, the lime in which has already been used, and then through stronger ones containing unslaked lime. Near the depilation pits there is often a flagged area where the hides are spread out and stretched. The hides are laid over a sloping pole or a large tree-trunk used as a 'horse', and the hair and remnants of flesh are scraped off. Basin 24, in which a deposit of lime was found, could have been a depilation pit of this kind. As we have seen, this basin was emptied from the bottom, and the solution used for the depilation was collected in the pit adjoining where it served as a weaker bath. When it was of no further use it was drawn up with buckets by way of the

---

[1] On the leather industry in ancient times, cf. *A History of Technology*, under the direction of Ch. Singer, II (1956), 147–87, *Leather*, by J. W. Waterer; 187–90, *A Note on Parchment* by H. Saxl. Above all R. J. Forbes, *Studies in Ancient Technology*, V (1957), 1–77, 'Leather in Antiquity'. For Palestine, cf. G. Dalman, *Arbeit und Sitte in Palästina*, V (1937), 185–95. The references in the literature of the Talmudic period have been assembled by S. Krauss, *Talmudische Archäologie*, II (1911), 259-66.

steps, and thrown into the gutter which drains away to the south. The paved surface round the edge of Basin 24 could have been used to stretch the hides, and the large cylindrical stones would have been 'horses' used in the process of scraping off the hair and flesh. The jar which was found laid, but not fixed, in the hollow space in the flagged area near Tank 23 could have contained some necessary ingredient for the actual work, or alternatively it could have been used to store drinking water for the workmen, since they could not drink the water from the basins where the hides were steeped.

The final process by which hides are turned into leather is the actual tanning. Strictly speaking it signifies that they are treated with tan, which is contained in the bark of oaks and other trees, or in gall-nuts, but other ingredients apart from vegetable tan can be used in the process. In particular pigeon dung and alum are both materials which have been used for tanning. The pit attached to the south corner of Basin 24, and fed by a special branch of the channel, could have been a tanning pit. The large basin at loc. 26 could have been used for rinsing the hides, but this purpose could have been equally well served by the tank at loc. 23. Again it may have been this tank that was used for the tanning. Here, as elsewhere, the hides would have been arranged in layers separated from one another by beds of crushed bark. We have seen that great care was taken here to ensure a gentle flow of water down into the basin. Presumably the reason for this was that it was important to the tanners for the whole pile to be impregnated evenly throughout, and right down to the bottom.

This interpretation, however, has to contend with serious difficulties. Both in the ancient tanneries which have been dis-covered,[1] and in those modern tanneries in which the traditional methods are continued,[2] the depilation pits and the tanning pits are small and numerous. This makes it possible to treat simul-

---

[1] Cf. the Roman tannery at Pompeii, which is contemporaneous with the installation at Feshkha. A. Mau, Pompeii. Its Life and Art, 2nd English edition (1907), p. 398, fig. 229.

[2] Here I may refer to the plans published by L. Brunot in Hespéris, Archives berbères et Bulletin de l'Institut des hautes études marocaines, III (1923), pl. I facing p. 84 (Tannery at Rabat), and by R. Le Tourneau, L. Paye, R. Guyot, ibid., XXI (1935), 173, fig. 2 (Tannery at Fès). I have described a tannery at Hebron in Revue biblique, LXVI (1959), 235–6.

taneously several lots of hides at different stages of preparation. Moreover, since the workers can put the hides in and take them out without going down into the pits it has the further effect of reducing danger from the corrosive fluids in the baths. Besides this, there is a second objection. Samples have been taken from the basins, pits, and channels, and submitted for examination by the Government Laboratory of Amman, the Department of Leather Industries of the University of Leeds, and the London Institute of Archaeology. All the analyses agree. The deposit from Basin 24 does indeed consist mainly of carbonate of calcium, a finding which agrees with our own observations and could provide support for our theory. In the other samples the proportion of carbonate of calcium is still important, and sand is also present. All this could be explained by the dissolving of the plaster coating, and the same explanation would also apply to Basin 24. On the other hand no trace of tannin has been recognized. Thus, in order to maintain our hypothesis, we would have to conclude that in these pits, penetrated as they have been by water and silt over a period of nearly two thousand years, every remnant of tannin has been oxidized and has disappeared.

This is not impossible. Moreover, in the judgement of two experts in tanning, residents in Jordan who have visited the excavations and are aware of the negative result of the analyses, it is still possible that this installation could have been used for treating hides. The specialists at the University of Leeds, on the contrary, regard it as reasonably certain that the basins at Feshkha were not used for the preparation of hides. The absence of tannin and of any organic element in the deposits analysed seems to them to point to this conclusion. However, they do recognize that the hypothesis of a tannery provides a good explanation of certain features: the position of the establishment near a spring, yet remote from the central buildings of Khirbet Qumran, the paved surfaces, and the stone 'horses'.[1]

One major objection to the hypothesis—the absence of tannin in the chemical analyses—would disappear if it were supposed

[1] J. B. Poole, R. Reed, 'The "Tannery" of 'Aïn Feshkha', *Palestine Exploration Quarterly* (1961), 114–23; 'The Preparation of Leather and Parchment by the Dead Sea Scrolls Community', *Technology and Culture*, III, 1 (1962), 1–26.

that this workplace was set up for the preparation not of leather but of parchment. In fact the technical difference between parchment and leather is that the former consists of untanned hide that has been dried, stretched on a frame, and pared thin with a scraping-knife.[1] But before undergoing these special treatments, through which it is turned into a skin suitable to be written on, the hide has to be subjected to the same preliminary processes as those used in the treatment of leather: repeated washings, bathings in lime, and depilation. These are precisely the processes for which the installations at Feshkha seem most suitable: the tank of running water, Basin 24, with its deposit of lime, the flagged pavement, and the cylindrical stones.

However, Professor F. E. Zeuner of the London Institute of Archaeology has subjected the samples to microscopic examination, and his findings reinforce the objections to the 'tannery' hypothesis already created by the plan and the chemical analyses. These samples do not contain any of the organic waste matter, especially hair, which we should find in pits where skins had been treated.[2] This seems to rule out the preparation of parchment no less than that of leather. F. E. Zeuner suggests another explanation: these basins were designed for rearing fish, which would have made a substantial contribution to the community's food supplies. This would satisfactorily explain the provision by which running water was made to circulate, and also the conduit at the bottom of Basin 24, enabling it to be emptied. In this way the larger fish could have been caught while the small fry were carried down into the pit adjoining, from which they could easily have been collected. A 'fish farm' of this kind is not impossible. In recent times it has actually been attempted in some basins fed by the small springs lying to the south of Khirbet Qumran, and if the enterprise has failed to prosper, that is because the elementary care necessary for it to succeed was neglected. However, this is not a very satisfactory way of accounting for the basins at Feshkha. For rearing fish it was unnecessary to coat the basins with plaster, and it would have been better not to do so, but to allow for the growth of the aquatic plants and insect life on which

---

[1] H. Saxl in *A History of Technology*, II, 187.

[2] F. E. Zeuner, 'Notes on Qumrân', *Palestine Exploration Quarterly* (1960), 27–36.

the fish could feed. These basins seem too small to have yielded any significant harvest to support a community, even a restricted one. If fish life had continued in them for any length of time some organic residue should have remained in them, and this is just as true of the rearing of fish as it is of the preparation of hides. Finally the hypothesis either fails to explain, or explains in an unsatisfactory manner, certain features, those in fact which constitute the distinctive characteristics of this installation: the pits in the two small paved rooms, the flagged surface, the cylindrical stones, and the complex water system, which suggest that the basins were designed for more than one purpose.

Thus, while the interpretation remains uncertain, the conclusion is established that this installation was planned for some industrial use. The minute detail in which it has been described here may seem excessive, but our intention has been to enable the reader either to evaluate the two solutions which have so far been proposed, or to discover a better one for himself.

The installation fell into disuse during Period III. The two openings at loc. 29, through which the water had been brought into the courtyard, were carefully stopped up, and thenceforward the water followed its natural flow outside the north wall of the enclosure.

To complete the description of the ruins of Feshkha one further feature must be noticed, a low wall of poor construction running north-eastwards from the north-west corner of the southern enclosure (Pl. xli). Its course has been traced for more than 200 m. It is likely that it joined on to the wall running southwards from Wadi Qumran, which had probably been built in the Israelite period.[1] The long boundary thus formed served to define the limits of the tract of land irrigated by the springs.

---

[1] Cf. pp. 59–60. These two walls were described accurately more than a century ago by E. G. Rey in his *Voyage dans le Haouran et aux bords de la mer Morte, exécuté pendant les années 1857 et 1858*, Paris (no date), 224–5: 'At ten minutes past two we cross the bed of Wadi Ghoumran, and almost at once the remains of a large wall appear on our left, separating the dry land from the marsh, which is covered with tall thickly-clumped reeds. Twenty minutes later this wall comes to an end, or rather disappears in the marsh, which seems to have encroached further upon the dry land in this area. Then we cross a tract of dried-up land which continues right to the foot of the mountain.

VIII. CONCLUSION

If the wall just referred to had been preserved throughout its length it would give concrete expression to the connection which certainly existed between the ruins of Feshkha and those of Khirbet Qumran. So far as their main periods are concerned they share the same history and were occupied by the same group. The establishment at Feshkha is less important, and is clearly a dependency of the central settlement of Khirbet Qumran. It is situated near a major spring, and at the boundary of a tract of land irrigated by other springs as well, and in which at least date-palms were cultivated. It consists of a building, a farm-building rather than a private dwelling, which has adjoining it an enclosure for livestock and basins used in some kind of industry. Feshkha, then, can be considered as an agricultural and industrial establishment used to benefit the community of Qumran.

It may seem paradoxical to speak of agriculture and industry in a terrain which is generally considered to have the character of a desert. Yet, contrary to what has been asserted,[1] the area of Qumran is neither uninhabitable nor totally devoid of natural resources.[2] In the course of our campaigns of excavation we saw flocks of sheep and goats passing by daily, and also camels, which browsed on the tufts of salt grass of the littoral plain and the scanty grass on the mountainside, and slaked their thirst at

'Shortly before arriving at our camping-ground a new wall appears, still on our left. It may be the continuation of the first. It is ten minutes to three when we alight at the spot where our tents are being pitched, about 200 metres from 'Aïn Feschkah.'

[1] H. Del Medico, *L'Énigme des manuscrits de la Mer Morte* (1957), 101–2, 107–8.

[2] On the flora and fauna of the Qumran area, cf. the observations of E. W. G. Masterman, published each year from 1901 to 1913 in the *Palestine Exploration Fund, Quarterly Statement*. These were made in the course of his visits for the purpose of recording the variations in level of the Dead Sea from the vicinity of 'Aïn Feshkha. On the economic possibilities of the area, cf. the somewhat optimistic estimates of W. R. Farmer, 'The Economic Basis of the Qumran Community', *Theologische Zeitschrift*, IX (1955), 295–308, with the 'Postscript', *ibid.* XII (1956), 56–8, and those of H. Bardtke, *Die Handschriften am Toten Meer*, II (1958), 12–17; idem, 'Zwischen chirbet Qumrān und 'en feschcha', *Theologische Literaturzeitung*, LXXXV (1960), 263–74. Cf. also *Revue biblique*, LXVI (1959), 95–8; S. Schulz, *Zeitschrift des deutschen Palästina Vereins*, LXXVI (1960), 65–70.

the spring of Feshkha or in the pools of Wadi Qumran. With a minimum of adaptation a palm-grove could be grown in the terrain irrigated by the springs, and we have positive signs that the date-palm was cultivated there in ancient times.[1] The littoral plain of the Dead Sea is unsuitable for the cultivation of cereals, but barley grows in the Buqei'a plain above Qumran, and corn-mills have been found in the Khirbeh.[2] The clumps of reeds which grow wild round the springs, especially near 'Ain Feshkha, are put to use by the people of Abu Dis, who make them into mats and baskets, as they were already doing half a century ago.[3] In ancient times the inhabitants of Khirbet Qumran and Fesh-kha made use of them for their roofs and in their weaving work. They exploited two products of the Dead Sea, certainly the salt, and perhaps the bitumen from it as well. It is well known that from time to time asphalt is emitted from the bed of this sea (the ancients used to call it the Lake of Asphalt) in an almost pure state, which then floats to the surface or is cast up on the banks.[4] In antiquity this bitumen gave rise to a lucrative trade, of which, for a time, the Nabataeans had a monopoly.[5] How far the community of Qumran profited from it we cannot say, but it must be pointed out that some pieces of this asphalt have been found at Khirbet Qumran, while a considerably larger quantity had been heaped up on one of the floors at Feshkha. As we have seen, some industries derived from agriculture or stock-rearing were practised at Feshkha, and there were several workshops at Khirbet Qumran. The fuel that was needed for these industries was obtained on the spot. To bake their bread the workers used brushwood and roots torn up from the area round the settlement, and the bushes growing in the area watered by the springs actually provide wood for the refugees in the camps at Jericho to this day.

[1] Cf. pp. 73–4.

[2] Cf. pp. 28–9.

[3] E. W. G. Masterman, *Palestine Exploration Fund, Quarterly Statement*, 1902, 166; 1904, 91–4.

[4] F. M. Abel, *Géographie de la Palestine*, I, 1933, 193–5. For the last observation of the phenomenon in 1952, cf. N. Glueck, *Bulletin of the American Schools of Oriental Research*, **131**, Oct. 1953, 15 and fig. 4. This occurs particularly at the time of earthquakes, as in 1834 and 1837 (according to Robinson), and 1927 (according to Abel).

[5] P. C. Hammond, 'The Nabataean Bitumen Industry at the Dead Sea', *Biblical Archaeologist*, xxii (1959), 40–8.

Certainly the resources of the area are very poor, but they do exist, and it is not impossible to live there. It was in fact inhabited in ancient times, as is proved by the Israelite installations discovered at Khirbet Qumran and at the foot of the plateau, the Roman military outpost at Khirbet Qumran, and the Byzantine hermitage at Feshkha. But, as we have seen, a more important phase of occupation was that which extended from the second half of the second century B.C. to A.D. 68. Evidence of it appears in the caves of the rock cliffs and the marl terrace alike, as well as in the buildings of Khirbet Qumran, the large cemetery adjoining, the building of Feshkha together with its annexes, and also in the way in which the tract of land which lies between Khirbet Qumran and Feshkha was put to use. These features cannot be disconnected from one another, and must be interpreted as a whole. The people who lived in the caves or in huts near the cliffs were the same as those who used to hold their assemblies at Khirbet Qumran. There they had their communal activities and their communal stores. They laboured in the workshops at Khirbet Qumran or on the farm at Feshkha. They were buried either in the main cemetery or in the subsidiary ones.

For a period of almost two centuries, therefore, a community lived in this abandoned region. Its importance in terms of numbers is difficult to establish. However, we must take into account the duration of this occupation, the number of the tombs, and the average life-span as determined from the skeletons which have been brought to light. From all these factors it can be estimated that even at the period of its greatest prosperity the group would not have numbered many more than 200 members.[1] It was an organized group, as is shown by the complex plan of the buildings and water supply, the number of places of common use, and the uniform arrangement of the main cemetery. We may go further when we recall the unique aspects in the form of burial and the special character of the large assembly room, with its additional function as a place for community meals, the remains of which were carefully buried.

[1] Slightly different estimates given in J. T. Milik, *Ten Years of Discovery in the Wilderness of Judaea*, 1959, 97: 'between 150 and 200'; W. R. Farmer, *Theologische Zeitschrift*, XI (1955), 304: 'a few hundred *regular* members'.

These are factors which, taken together, suggest that the community was religious in character, with special ritual observances of its own.

Archaeology can proceed thus far without either failing in scientific method or overstepping its proper limits, even though it can be concerned only with material remains. But it still remains for us to compare the conclusions arrived at so far with the written documents, and then attempt an historical interpretation.

APPENDIX TO CHAPTER II

At the time when we explored the cliffs in 1952 we had taken note of the two southernmost caves, situated on the promontory of Ras Feshkha which falls abruptly into the sea. These caves had shown evidence of having been occupied at the same time as the caves with manuscripts and the buildings of Qumran. When we extended our exploration a little further to the south we did not discover anything belonging to that period, and we concluded that Ras Feshkha, which constitutes a natural barrier, marked the southernmost boundary of the area occupied by the community.

Now, however, in the light of more recent explorations which have been made on the western shores of the Dead Sea, it is necessary to revise this conclusion. In 1953 an expedition of Belgian archaeologists under the direction of R. De Langhe discovered a small ruin called Khirbet Mazin about three kilometres to the south of Ras Feshkha and on the northern edge of the Kedron delta, very close to the actual shore-line. It is a rectangular building, but only one trial sounding was made, at the wide entrance on the side nearest the sea. In December 1960 and January 1961 an expedition was mounted by Mr. John Allegro to discover the treasures mentioned in the Copper Scrolls. Although in other respects it was a total failure, Khirbet Mazin was included in the programme, and R. De Langhe was invited to excavate this site which he had been the first to place on record. A preliminary report has been published,[1] but the

---

[1] H. E. Stutchbury, G. R. Nicholl, 'Khirbet Mazin', *Annual of the Department of Antiquities of Jordan*, VI–VII (1962), 96–103, pls. xviii–xxiii.

excavator provides neither descriptions nor illustrations of any of the objects discovered. It can only be conjectured that the building was erected during the Roman period, perhaps in connection with the commercial exploitation of salt from the Dead Sea. It was reoccupied to a slight extent in the Byzantine period. I myself visited the site in 1956, and I did not find any evidence to justify the theory that it was connected with the installations at Qumran and Feshkha.

The problem arises in a different form in the case of another site, lying six or seven kilometres further south and near the spring of 'Ain el-Ghuweir. Here too, incidentally, remains have survived from the Israelite period. A new road has recently been built linking 'Ain Feshkha with En-Gedi, and at the time of this construction the Roman remains at this other site were recognized and excavated.[1] M. P. Bar-Adon has laid bare the remains of a rectangular building, measuring 19.50 × 43.00 m., with other walls joined to it. Two distinct periods of occupation can be discerned, the relevant strata being separated by a layer of burnt material. From this layer of destruction the following coins have been recovered: five undated coins of Herod the Great, one of Herod Archelaus, and one of Agrippa I, belonging to the commonest type, that with the three ears of corn and the parasol, struck in the year VI (A.D. 42/43). The pottery recovered from this building, though in a somewhat shattered state, corresponds to these dates. It has its counterparts at Qumran and Feshkha, especially among the examples from Period II. It is, perhaps, justifiable to assign certain forms to as early a date as the end of the Hasmonean age, but this is not certain, and is not supported by the discovery of any coins of that period.

About 800 m. to the north of this building a small cemetery was identified, and the contents of some twenty of its tombs were removed. They included the remains of 12 men, 7 women, and a boy of seven. With one exception all these tombs were orientated from north to south with the head of the dead person to the south. They are identical in form with the tombs of the main

[1] P. Bar-Adon, 'Chronique archéologique', *Revue biblique*, LXXVII (1970), 398–400; *Idem*, 'Another Settlement of the Judaean Desert Sect at 'Aïn Ghuweir on the Dead Sea', *Eretz-Israel*, x (1971), 72–89 (in Hebrew with a summary in English).

cemetery at Qumran. Such remains of pottery as have been found in the filling of the pits show signs of being contemporaneous with the building which has been described. One of the tombs was unusual in that it contained a jar inscribed with the name *yhwḥnn*. It is tempting to see a connection between the cemetery and building here and the installations at Qumran and Feshkha. The tombs are of the same type and were used for Jewish burials, as is shown by the evidence of the inscribed jar. The pottery types, or at least some of them, have their counterparts at Qumran. The building could have served as a place of assembly for the members of a group which lived in scattered caves or shelters round about, once more as at Qumran. This is one possible conclusion. At the same time, however, it should be noticed that the pottery forms most characteristic of Period I*b* at Khirbet Qumran are missing here, and, furthermore, that there are no coins earlier than Herod the Great, and none of the last Procurators or of the Jewish Revolt. In view of the small number of coins recovered this *argumentum ex silentio* carries no very great weight, but it could serve to indicate that the installation at 'Ain Ghuweir was begun later, and terminated earlier, than that at Qumran. It will also be noticed that we have no absolute proof of any connection having existed between the building and the cemetery laid out some 800 m. to the north of it. A further point is that the group involved here, having installed themselves some 15 km. southwards from Qumran, and about 12 km. to the south of the natural barrier of Ras Feshkha, could not in any case have had any very close connection with the community centre. Finally no document of the type found at Qumran has been found either in the ruins themselves or in the caves nearby. An excavation has been made of one of these latter, situated above 'Ain Turaba and near 'Ain el-Ghuweir. It was never anything more than a Byzantine hermitage.[1] In the absence of any stronger proof it may perhaps be suggested that it is rash to apply the designation 'Essene'[2] to the building excavated near 'Ain el-Ghuweir or to the cemetery which may have been attached to it. We should bear in mind that particularly during the second Iron Age and the Roman period the

---

[1] Ian Blake, 'Chronique archéologique', *Revue biblique*, LXXIII (1966), 566.
[2] P. Bar-Adon in the articles quoted in n. 1, p. 88.

west bank of the Dead Sea was more thickly populated than we have been accustomed to imagine.

The problem of whether there was ever an Essene settlement above En-Gedi will be discussed at a later stage in connection with the relevant passage from Pliny the Elder.[1]

[1] Cf. below, pp. 133 ff.

III

THE RUINS AND THE TEXTS

HAVING presented the material findings of the archaeological exploration of Khirbet Qumran and the Qumran area, it remains for us to establish what bearing these discoveries have upon the texts and upon history. All that is necessary has already been said about the final periods of occupation. The reason why the Romans maintained a military outpost at Khirbet Qumran after the destruction of the buildings is that they needed to watch over the shores of the Dead Sea at least up to the fall of Masada in A.D. 73. Light is thrown upon the use of the ruins of Khirbet Qumran and Feshkha by the rebels of the Second Jewish War by the documents of Murabba'at, which show that the desert of Judaea was the final refuge of the insurgents. A connection has been established between the small Byzantine settlement at Feshkha and an anecdote related by John Moschus.[1] There is no need to recapitulate these findings. But to throw still more light upon the Israelite occupation of the area, and above all to establish the connection between the ruins and the documents discovered in the caves nearby, we must turn to the Old Testament.

I. THE ISRAELITE OCCUPATION

At the end of the list of towns of Judah recorded in the Book of Joshua six 'towns' are included situated 'in the wilderness': Bet-ha-'Araba, Middin, Sekaka, Nibshan, 'Ir-hammelaḥ, and En-Gedi (Josh. 15: 61–2). The last-named of these towns may confidently be located at Tell el-Jurn, beside the spring of 'Ain Jidi near the Dead Sea shore, and some thirty kilometres to the south of Khirbet Qumran. The first of them, Bet-ha-'Araba, should most probably be located near the spring of 'Ain el-Gharabeh, to the south-east of Jericho. Hence the towns are

---

[1] Cf. above, p. 75.

enumerated from north to south, and even before the excavations at Khirbet Qumran M. Noth had suggested that this site should be identified with ʿIr-hammelaḥ, the 'City of Salt', which we should look for somewhere to the north of En-Gedi and on the shore of the Dead Sea, the 'Sea of Salt' of the Old Testament.[1] At the time of the first clearances at Khirbet Qumran Noth withdrew this suggestion because they had yielded nothing earlier than the Greco-Roman period.[2] But as the work progressed his hypothesis has proved justified, and we have described the Israelite building, the basic elements of which were found beneath the community settlement of Khirbet Qumran.[3] Hence the identification proposed by Noth is very probably correct,[4] and it is confirmed by the researches of F. M. Cross and J. T. Milik in the plain of the Buqeiʿa above Khirbet Qumran.[5] They explored three sites which, both in their plans and in the pottery they yielded, showed analogies with the plan and the pottery of the Israelite settlement at Khirbet Qumran. Moreover, the three sites can be identified with the three remaining towns in the list in Joshua. If we adhere strictly to the geographical order from north to south we arrive at the following precise identifications: Middin = Khirbet Abu Ṭabaq, Sekaka = Khirbet es-Samra, Nibshan = Khirbet el-Maqari. The ancient way leading down from the Buqeiʿa to Khirbet Qumran[6] may perhaps derive from this period, and would have ensured that the three settlements in the Buqeiʿa were able to communicate with that on the littoral plain. Even before the time when the Israelite buildings were destroyed to make room for the later building work at Khirbet Qumran, there was, as we have said, an earlier structure of the same general type, though only inhabited for a short time, and the traces of this are discernible at the foot of the

[1] M. Noth, *Das Buch Josua* (1938), 72.

[2] *Das Buch Josua*, 2nd edn. (1953), 100.

[3] Above, pp. 1–3.

[4] The arguments have been expounded by Noth himself, 'Der alttestamentliche Name der Siedlung auf chirbet ḳumrān', *Zeitschrift des Deutschen Palästina-Vereins*, LXXI (1955), 111–23.

[5] F. M. Cross, 'A Footnote to Biblical History', *Biblical Archaeologist*, XIX (1956), 12–17; F. M. Cross and J. T. Milik, 'Explorations in the Judaean Buqêʿah', *Bulletin of the American Schools of Oriental Research*, 142 (April 1956), 5–17.

[6] Above, pp. 5–6.

terrace at Qumran.[1] A further feature which we can assign to the Israelite occupation is the long wall running southwards from Wadi Qumran to mark the boundary of the tract of land irrigated by the springs.[2] Finally it should be noticed that a few pieces of Israelite pottery have been discovered in some of the caves in the rock cliffs, showing that they were put to use during the same period.

Recently the identification of Khirbet Qumran with one of the towns in the list of Josh. 15: 61–2 has once more been called in question. In the Copper Scroll, 3Q 15, Sekaka is mentioned four times as a place, but also as a valley and in connection with an aqueduct.[3] It seems likely that in this passage Sekaka is the name assigned to Wadi Qumran, probably throughout its entire length. In the light of this some authors have concluded that the Israelite name for Khirbet Qumran was Sekaka, and not, as we have stated, the 'City of Salt', 'Ir-hammelaḥ.[4] However there is another town, Khirbet es-Samra, lying at the beginning of Wadi Qumran in the Buqeiʿa, where it constitutes a most prominent site. There is every possibility that this was Sekaka. Moreover the 'City of Salt' should be on the edge of the sea, where Qumran is situated.[5] It is true that there is now a rival to Qumran: between ʿAin Ghuweir and ʿAin Turaba the ruins of two buildings belonging to the Israelite period have been excavated.[6] If Sekaka is indeed Khirbet Qumran these ruins could be those of the 'City of Salt', for in the list in Josh. 15: 61–2 this is assigned a place between Sekaka and En-Gedi. The main objection to these new theories is that they leave the most notable site in the Buqeiʿa unnamed, for surely the two settlements of Khirbet es-Samra and Khirbet Qumran, separated as they are by a distance of seven or eight kilometres, would each have had their own name even if they were linked by the same wadi. And it is normal practice in such a situation for the site near the beginning of the wadi to bear the same name as the wadi itself.

[1] pp. 58–9. [2] pp. 59–60.
[3] 3Q15, iv. 13; v. 2, 5, 13; cf. J. T. Milik, Discoveries in the Judaean Desert, III (1962), 263–4, 288–90.
[4] J. M. Allegro, *The Treasure of the Copper Scroll* (1960), 68–74, 144–5.
[5] F. M. Cross, *The Ancient Library of Qumran . . .*, 2nd edn. (1961), 54 n. 4.
[6] I. Blake, 'Chronique archéologique', *Revue biblique*, LXXIII (1966), 565–6; P. Bar-Adon, *ibid.* LXXVII (1970), 399–400.

Among the materials collected at Khirbet Qumran and in the caves nothing appears to be earlier than the eighth century B.C., and this date suggests that there may be some connection here with what is recorded in 2 Chr. 26: 10 about the activities of Uzziah (781–740 B.C.), who had large herds, loved the soil, 'built towers (*migdâlîm*) in the wilderness and hewed out many cisterns'. It is true that F. M. Cross assigns a slightly earlier date to the three settlements in the Buqei‘a and suggests that they should be attributed to Jehoshaphat (870–848 B.C.), for according to 2 Chr. 17: 12 he 'built in Judah fortresses (*birâniyyôt*, equivalent to *migdâlîm*) and store-cities'.[1] However, from the published accounts the pottery of these three sites does not seem to be earlier than that of Khirbet Qumran,[2] and the position of all the sites 'in the wilderness' accords better with the passage concerning Uzziah. However, one point must be conceded: the pottery from the first Israelite settlement at the foot of the plateau of Qumran is a little earlier, probably belonging to the ninth century B.C., and hence could go back to the reign of Jehoshaphat.

These findings have a special interest of their own in determining the date of the list of the towns of Judah recorded in the Book of Joshua. But they represent only one small element in a complex problem, in which not only literary criticism, but the history and archaeology of all the towns in the list have a part to play. Not all the sections in the list need necessarily reflect one and the same historical situation, and the minor settlements of the Buqei‘a and Qumran could have had a distinct history of their own. It would fit in well with the historical evidence if we assigned their foundation and brief history to a period of power and economic prosperity such as the reigns of Jehoshaphat and of Uzziah are both known to have been.[3]

[1] *Bulletin of the American Schools . . ., loc. cit.* 17.

[2] Previously the same opinion was upheld by Y. Aharoni in *Vetus Testamentum* IX (1959), 242. Subsequently, however, he has opted for the reign of Jehoshaphat, *The Land of the Bible* (1967), 295–7.

[3] Concerning these lists of the towns of Judah the essential studies are the following: A. Alt, 'Judas Gaue unter Josia', *Palästina Jahrbuch*, XXI (1925), 100–16, reproduced in his *Kleine Schriften* II (1955), 276–88 (under Josiah). His position is followed by M. Noth in his commentary on Joshua, and in *The History of Israel*, 2nd edn. (1960), 273; F. M. Cross and G. E. Wright, 'The Boundary and Province Lists of the Kingdom of Juda', *Journal of*

II. THE 'DEAD SEA SCROLLS' AND THE CAVES

But the most important and best documented period in the history of Qumran is that during which it was occupied by a community. This lasted from the second half of the second century B.C. to A.D. 68, with an interruption lasting several decades at the end of the first century B.C. Moreover the most sensational discovery made in this area is that of the manuscripts found in the caves. The connection between the manuscripts, the caves, and the ruins must be determined, and once this is established it must be shown how the two kinds of evidence, the documentary and the archaeological, each throw light upon the other. Shortly after the initial discoveries certain doubts were expressed, and in a few of the studies which have since been published they are still maintained. In order to dispel them we shall begin by showing that these documents were indeed found in the caves at Qumran, that they are ancient themselves, and that they were deposited in the caves in ancient times.

1. *The Manuscripts Were Found in the Caves*

The initial discovery was made by some Bedouin in 1947 in Cave 1. This cave was identified and excavated by the archaeologists in 1949. They collected a number of further fragments from it, some of which belong to manuscripts which had been sold by the Bedouin as having come from this actual cave.[1]

In February 1952 the Bedouin discovered Cave 2 and we arrived after them. Every nook and cranny of the cave had been emptied, but we still found two written fragments in the debris thrown outside it by the clandestine excavators. We then explored the rock cliffs and discovered Cave 3. Its mouth had been blocked and the Bedouin did not know of its existence. But it

---

Biblical Literature, LXXV (1956), 202–26 (under Jehoshaphat). Their conclusions are followed by J. Bright, *A History of Israel* (1959), 233; Z. Kallai-Kleinmann, 'The Town Lists of Judah, Simeon, Benjamin, and Dan', *Vetus Testamentum* VIII (1958), 134–60, and 'Note . . .', *ibid.*, IX (1959), 223–7 (under Hezekiah); Y. Aharoni, 'The Province-List of Judah', *Vetus Testamentum*, IX (1959), 225–46 (under Uzziah), but cf. also the same author's *The Land of the Bible* (1967), 295–7 (under Jehoshaphat).

[1] Cf. D. Barthélemy and J. T. Milik, Discoveries in the Judaean Desert, I, *Qumran Cave I* (1955), 4 and, with regard to the texts, 5, 33, 35.

was from this cave that the Copper Scrolls and some texts written on skin and papyrus came.

In September 1952 the Bedouin discovered Cave 4 in the marl terrace. We ousted the Bedouin, and ourselves unearthed some hundreds of fragments. The majority belong to the same manuscripts as those from which other pieces sold by the Bedouin derive.[1] Very close to Cave 4 we then discovered Cave 5, which no one had previously recognized, and which contained fragments from more than fifteen manuscripts buried under a barren deposit more than one metre in depth. The small cave known as Cave 6 was discovered by the Bedouin almost at the same time as Cave 4, and from this our workmen took some further fragments of writing.

During the excavation campaign at Khirbet Qumran in 1955 we identified Caves 7 to 10 on the flanks of the marl terrace on which the ruins are situated. Up to that point no one had suspected their existence. Although they had almost entirely eroded away and fallen into the ravine they still contained some further fragments of writing on skin and papyrus.

Finally in 1956 the Bedouin opened up Cave 11 and took certain important manuscripts from it. We followed them and ourselves collected some fragments from it.

All the caves in the Qumran area where the Bedouin say they discovered manuscripts have been identified by us, and from each of them we have taken at least some written fragments. We ourselves discovered Caves 3, 5, 7, 8, 9, and 10, which contained fragments of the same type. It is astonishing that as late as 1954 R. Lacheman still found it possible to write: 'The fact still remains that not a single document has been found by an archaeologist',[2] and that as late as 1957, with reference to the scrolls of Cave 1, S. Zeitlin was still able to ask: 'Were they indeed discovered by Beduin, or were they planted in the cave to be discovered later, and hence the entire discovery is a hoax?'[3] The answer is simple: these manuscripts certainly come from the cave subsequently explored by the archaeologists, since the latter collected from it fragments deriving from the same

[1] F. M. Cross, *The Ancient Library of Qumran . . .*, 2nd edn. (1961), 26.
[2] *Jewish Quarterly Review*, n.s. XLIV (1953–4), 290.
[3] *Ibid.* n.s. XLVII (1956–7), 267.

documents. But the manuscripts themselves were discovered by the Bedouin, who did not have any reason for 'planting' them there in order to 'discover' them for themselves. The same answer applies to all the caves where the Bedouin were the first to arrive. The other caves, those discovered by the archaeologists, were unknown to the Bedouin. They had been blocked up since ancient times, and no one could have 'planted' in them the manuscripts they were found to contain.

2. *The Manuscripts are Ancient*

All the manuscripts and fragments, both those coming from the Bedouin and those discovered by the archaeologists, are ancient. Even before the excavation of Cave 1, and without any knowledge of the archaeological context in which they were discovered, the antiquity of the manuscripts had been established by palaeography. As soon as he saw the first documents, in November 1947, E. L. Sukenik recognized their similarity to the inscriptions on the ossuaries of the first century B.C. to the first century A.D.[1] As soon as he received the photographs W. F. Albright concluded that the great scroll of Isaiah dated from the second century B.C.[2] The more the texts were published and studied the more these conclusions have been confirmed and developed. In Cave 4 fragments of Samuel and Jeremiah have been discovered which go back to the end of the third century B.C.,[3] as well as fragments of Ecclesiastes belonging to the middle of the second century B.C.,[4] a little earlier than the scroll of Isaiah of Cave 1. The most recent manuscripts of Qumran are certainly earlier than the documents of the Second Revolt, A.D. 132–5, discovered by us at Murabba'at[5] and others from the same period found in the caves excavated by the Israelites between En-Gedi and Masada.[6] Taking these two

[1] E. L. Sukenik, *The Dead Sea Scrolls of the Hebrew University* (1955), 14.
[2] *Bulletin of the American Schools of Oriental Research*, **110** (Apr. 1948), 3.
[3] F. M. Cross, 'The Oldest Manuscripts from Qumran', *Journal of Biblical Literature*, LXXIV (1955), 147–72.
[4] J. Muilenburg, 'A Qoheleth Scroll from Qumran', *Bulletin of the American Schools . . .*, **135** (Oct. 1954), 20–8.
[5] P. Benoit, J. T. Milik, and R. de Vaux, Discoveries in the Judaean Desert, II, *Les Grottes de Murabba'ât* (1961).
[6] Provisionally, N. Avigad, Y. Aharoni, P. Bar-Adon, Y. Yadin, 'The Expedition to the Judaean Desert 1960', *Israel Exploration Journal*, XI (1961),

dates as their limits on either side, the palaeographers have classified the Qumran manuscripts chronologically, and have assigned them a place within the broader framework of Hebrew palaeography and epigraphy.[1]

The date assigned to the Qumran manuscripts has been confirmed by the discoveries at Masada. The ostraca and the writings, both biblical and non-biblical, discovered in the excavations there are in the same script as those of Qumran, and none of them can be later than A.D. 73, when the fortress fell at the hands of the Romans.[2]

Further proof of antiquity is provided by the character of the biblical text exhibited by these documents. It appears both in the biblical manuscripts themselves and in the quotations from the bible in the non-biblical ones. Side by side with texts which are proto-masoretic, the Qumran series includes witnesses to the Samaritan recension, as well as to the Hebrew original from which the Septuagint was translated.[3] Such witnesses belong to a

1–52; Id., 'The Expedition to the Judaean Desert 1961', *Israel Exploration Journal*, XII (1962), 167–262; Y. Yadin, *The Finds from the Bar-Kokhba Period in the Cave of the Letters* (1963); Y. Yadin, *Bar-Kokhba, The Rediscovery of the Legendary Hero of the Last Jewish Revolt against Imperial Rome* (1971).

[1] Cf. above all S. A. Birnbaum, *The Qumrân (Dead Sea) Scrolls and Palaeography*, Supplementary Studies, 13–14 to *Bulletin of the American Schools of Oriental Research* (1952); N. Avigad, 'The Palaeography of the Dead Sea Scrolls', *Aspects of the Dead Sea Scrolls*, Scripta Hierosolymitana, IV (1958), 56–87; J. T. Milik, *Ten Years of Discovery in the Wilderness of Judaea* (1959), 133–6.

[2] Y. Yadin, *Masada, First Season of Excavations, 1963–1964* (1965), 103–15; Id., *The Ben Sira Scroll from Masada* (1965); Id., *Masada. Herod's Fortress and the Zealots' Last Stand* (1966), 168–91.

[3] Cf. in particular W. F. Albright, 'New Light on Early Recensions of the Hebrew Bible', *Bulletin of the American Schools . . .*, **140** (Dec. 1955), 27–33; M. Greenberg, 'The Stabilization of the Text of the Hebrew Bible', *Journal of the American Oriental Society*, LXXVI (1956), 157–67; P. W. Skehan, 'The Qumran Manuscripts and Textual Criticism', *Volume of Congress, Strasbourg 1956*, Supplements to *Vetus Testamentum*, IV (1957), 148–60; F. M. Cross, *The Ancient Library of Qumrân . . .*, 2nd edn. (1961), 168–94; H. M. Orlinsky, 'Qumran and the Present State of Old Testament Studies: The Septuagint Text', *Journal of Biblical Literature*, LXXVIII (1959), 26–33; D. Barthélemy, *Les Devanciers d'Aquila*, Supplements to *Vetus Testamentum*, X (1963); F. M. Cross, 'The History of the Biblical Text in the Light of Discoveries in the Judaean Desert', *Harvard Theological Review*, LVII (1964), 281–99; S. Talmon, 'Aspects of the Textual Transmission of the Bible in the Light of the Qumrân Manuscripts', *Textus*, IV (1964), 95–132; P. Wernberg-Møller, 'The Contribution

time when the text of the Old Testament was still in a fluid state, and when several textual traditions were in existence side by side, a state prior to the fixing of the masoretic text which, by contrast, is the text exhibited by the manuscripts deposited in the caves of Murabba'at during the Second Revolt.

These conclusions have recently been confirmed by a physico-chemical analysis. Fragments from the Qumran and Murabba'at manuscripts which did not contain writing were sent for examination by the Department of Leather Industries at the University of Leeds. Fragments of parchment, when submitted to progressive heat, begin to shrink, and the more ancient the parchment the lower the temperature at which this takes place. On this basis the temperature of shrinkage of the fragments from Murabba'at and Qumran was determined and compared with that of fragments of parchment or untanned hide of known date: an untanned skin from Egypt of about 1300 B.C., some Aramaic documents of the fifth century B.C., and a series of English parchments ranging from the twelfth century A.D. down to modern times. All the samples thus treated fell into place within the temperature curve according to their respective ages. The Qumran fragments clearly come after the documents of the fifth century B.C., just before those of Murabba'at, and well before the parchments ranging from the twelfth century down to our own times.[1]

3. *These Manuscripts were Deposited in the Caves in Ancient Times*

The approximate date of the manuscripts as arrived at independently by palaeography, textual criticism, and physico-chemical analysis accords well with the date assigned by archaeology to the occupation of the caves where these manuscripts were

of the *Hodayot* to Biblical Textual Criticism', *ibid.*, 133–75; P. W. Skehan, 'The Biblical Scrolls from Qumrân and the Text of the Old Testament', *The Biblical Archaeologist*, xxviii (1965), 87–100; M. H. Goshen-Gottstein, 'The Psalms Scroll (11QPsᵃ): A Problem of Canon and Text', *Textus*, v (1966), 22–33; F. M. Cross, 'The Contribution of the Qumrân Discoveries to the Study of the Biblical Text', *Israel Exploration Journal*, xvi (1966), 81–95; *Bibel und Qumran. Beiträge zur Erforschung der Beziehungen zwischen Bibel- und Qumranwissenschaft. Hans Bardtke zum 22.9.1966*, ed. S. Wagner (1968).

[1] D. Burton, J. B. Poole, and R. Reed, 'A New Approach to the Dating of the Dead Sea Scrolls', *Nature*, **184** (15 Aug. 1959), 533–4.

discovered. It is reasonable to conclude that the manuscripts were deposited in the caves at the time of the occupation, and this conclusion is confirmed by other proofs.

The physical state of the manuscripts shows that they were deposited in the caves in ancient times. Almost all of them are much damaged and show traces of having been buried over a very long period in a place which was sometimes humid or subject to the attacks of rodents, insects, or worms. These findings have been contested by H. Del Medico, who concludes, solely from an examination of the photographs, that some of the manuscripts were deliberately burned or torn up, and furthermore that they were neither damaged by humidity since the caves are dry, nor gnawed by rats since rats do not live at Qumran.[1] Yet it is certain from the study of the manuscripts themselves and from direct knowledge of the area that the black marks which he takes for burning are the result of the skin having decomposed through being subjected to humidity, and that rats are very much at home at Qumran.[2]

The fact that the manuscripts were deposited in ancient times is equally borne out by their position in the caves. To confine ourselves to the most striking instances noticed by the archaeologists, the fragments from Caves 7 to 10 had evidently been deposited before the erosion or the collapses which carried away the greater part of these caves. The fragments from Cave 5 were lying under more than one metre of natural deposit. The many fragments recovered by us from Cave 4 went right down to the original floor of the cave and were coated with a marl sediment which had accumulated and solidified over a long period.[3]

---

[1] H. Del Medico, 'L'état des manuscrits de Qumrân I', *Vetus Testamentum*, VII (1957), 127–38; Id., *L'Énigme des Manuscrits de la Mer Morte* (1957), 47–63, 73, 75.

[2] Cf. *Revue biblique*, LXVI (1959), 93.

[3] As we have already said, many of the fragments come from manuscripts the remains of which were recovered by the Bedouin from the upper levels of the rubbish with which the cave was filled. It may be added that, apart from the damage caused by natural agents and animals, a number of these fragments show signs of having been torn by human hands. These mutilations, together with the fact that fragments from the same manuscripts had been scattered about, show that the cave had been pillaged in ancient times, and before the deposit of marl had invaded the cave and sealed them off. In view of the closeness of Cave 4 to the ruins of Qumran there can hardly be any

According to the Bedouin the major scrolls of the first discovery were wrapped in cloths. S. Zeitlin raises the objection that the archaeologists never saw the manuscripts wrapped up in this way.[1] This is true, but we have found a scroll fragment, unfortunately reduced to a solid black mass by humidity, wrapped up in one of these cloths.[2] However this may be, the cloths themselves, found at the same time as the manuscripts, must be considered to belong roughly to the same time as that at which the manuscripts were left in the caves until the contrary is proved. Some of them have been subjected to carbon-14 tests. The date which these yielded is A.D. 33, with a margin of error of 200 years. While we may feel some amusement at this margin, and feel that it shows the imprecision of carbon-14 as a method of dating,[3] it still remains true that there are limits to this imprecision, and that the process would not have yielded a date in the Roman period for cloths belonging to modern times.[4]

With the exception of Cave 5, which did not contain any sherds, pottery was recovered from all the other caves at the same time as the manuscripts. According to the Bedouin's version the first major documents were contained in jars. S. Zeitlin once more objects[5] that the archaeologists did not see the manuscripts enclosed in the jars. Again this is true, but they did see a fragment of scroll wrapped in cloth and sticking to the upper part of a broken jar.[6] The only point which I am insisting on here is that there were both manuscripts and pottery in the caves. Of course this does not mean that the manuscripts must necessarily be contemporaneous with the pottery. Even if we

doubt that the depredation here is to be ascribed to the Roman soldiers who occupied the ruins. It follows that the time at which the manuscripts were abandoned is earlier than the Roman occupation, the precise date of which we are about to establish on different grounds. We shall encounter the same sequence of events at Murabba'at. Here too the biblical texts were found in a mutilated condition in caves which had been occupied first by the Jewish rebels and then by Roman soldiers. Cf. Discoveries in the Judaean Desert, II (1961), 48.

[1] S. Zeitlin, *The Dead Sea Scrolls and Modern Scholarship* (1956), x.

[2] G. L. Harding in Discoveries in the Judaean Desert, I, *Qumran Cave I* (1955), 7 and pl. i, 8–10.

[3] S. Zeitlin, *The Dead Sea Scrolls* . . ., 88.

[4] Cf. p. 50.

[5] *The Dead Sea Scrolls* . . ., x and 86.

[6] Cf. *Qumran Cave I*, 7 and pl. i, 8.

admit, as I do, that some of the manuscripts were preserved in some of the jars,[1] it still remains a possibility that ancient manuscripts could have been put into new jars or conversely that later manuscripts could have been placed in older ones. It also remains a fact that not all the manuscripts were placed in jars (Caves 4 and 5 provide clear instances to the contrary), and theoretically possible that later manuscripts could have been deposited in a place already containing ancient pottery. But the latter seems to be excluded in the present instance. H. Del Medico raises the question: 'Who does not have some plate or other piece of pottery at his home which belonged to his grandparents?'[2] Obviously this is true, but Del Medico certainly has other plates besides those of his grandfather at his house. Now the pottery recovered from the caves is extremely plentiful: at least 50 jars and as many lids, at least 3 bowls, one pot, one juglet, and four lamps in Cave 1, a dozen jars, one lid, and three bowls in Cave 2, 20 jars, 26 lids, and two jugs in Cave 3 etc. All this pottery belongs to the Hellenistic and Roman period, and there is nothing from later periods. When we reflect that the manuscripts are numerous and the pottery plentiful, that the manuscripts constitute a homogeneous group, and that the pottery belongs to a single period, it is difficult to resist the conclusion that the manuscripts were deposited or abandoned in the caves at the same time as the pottery. The only possible exception which I would allow is that of the Copper Scroll, a point which I shall explain at a later stage.

III. THE MANUSCRIPTS AND THE COMMUNITY OF QUMRAN

We have seen that apart from the eleven manuscript caves some twenty further caves have been identified in the rock cliffs and that they contain pottery of identical type but no written fragments. Possibly no manuscripts were ever hidden in these caves. Possibly they did contain manuscripts but they have not been

---

[1] This method of conserving documents is attested by a number of examples from ancient times. Cf. R. de Vaux, *Revue biblique*, LVI (1949), 591–2; J. T. Milik, *Biblica*, XXXI (1950), 504–8; B. Couroyer, *Revue biblique*, LXII (1955), 76–81.

[2] *L'Énigme des Manuscrits de la mer Morte*, 15 n. 1.

preserved. What is certain, however, is that these caves were utilized at the same period as the manuscript caves.[1] We have established that the utilization of the caves was contemporaneous with, and dependent upon, the occupation by the community of Khirbet Qumran. The caves were used either as living quarters or as storage- or hiding-places for the members of the community who lived at Khirbet Qumran or in the surrounding area.[2] The final point which we now have to make is that the manuscripts are approximately of the same period as the pottery in the caves and that they were abandoned there at the same time as that pottery. The conclusion cannot be resisted that the source of these manuscripts was the community installed in the Qumran area. It is natural that in the ruins of Khirbet Qumran, exposed as they were to the weather, texts written on skin or papyrus should have failed to survive. But in the ruins themselves inscriptions have been found written on ostraca or pots, in particular a sherd bearing a complete alphabet, the exercise of a pupil-scribe.[3] If we allow for the difference in the materials, the writing is the same as that of the documents. The discoveries in the caves provide supporting proof. Brief inscriptions on one jar from Cave 4, another from Cave 7, and an ostracon from Cave 10 exhibit the same writing as the inscriptions found in the Khirbeh.

Thus, one hypothesis which we have already discussed can be definitely excluded,[4] namely that the manuscript caves were *genizôt*, places where manuscripts of unknown provenance, and without any connection with the occupation of Khirbet Qumran, were discarded. This does not, in itself, rule out the hypothesis that these caves may have been used as *genizôt* for the community of Qumran itself. This is an important point. If this hypothesis were true, the documents in the caves would be texts rejected by the community, and could not be used to determine its ways of thinking and living. But it is an unlikely hypothesis. We might accept that the community had a *genizah* (supposing that such an institution already existed at this period in so elaborate a form, even though we have no evidence of this), but what we cannot admit is that it had eleven *genizôt*. Moreover, in view of the fact that the state of the manuscripts

---

[1] Cf. pp. 49–53.
[3] Cf. *Revue biblique*, LXI (1954), pl. xxª.
[2] pp. 53–7.
[4] pp. 55–6.

is the same throughout, that the different groups are made up of the same types of material, and that the same works recur in several different caves, it must be recognized that none of the caves is a *genizah* and that all the works derive from the community and were accepted by it.

Arguing against those who consider these caves as *genizôt*, and deny that there was any connection between the manuscripts and Khirbet Qumran, Éd. Dhorme has taken the position that the buildings of Khirbet Qumran were occupied only by 'a college of scribes or copyists, and that their work, which was also their livelihood, consisted in re-copying primarily the biblical texts, but also other extracts from religious literature'.[1] However, it is improbable that scribes would have chosen to set up house at Qumran solely for the purpose of copying manuscripts there, and unlikely that their 'college' would have taken up such a large range of buildings, led to the use of some thirty caves, and filled a cemetery of more than a thousand tombs. Finally it is improbable that if they copied documents for the purpose of selling them, the documents would have been discovered here in so great a number. As R. Dussaud puts it, 'Is it conceivable that the scribes of the so-called scriptorium of Qumran would have toiled over this mass of documents without any further reward than that of burying them in caves which are, for the most part, uninhabitable?'[2]

Certainly manuscripts were copied in the *scriptorium* of Qumran, and in the case of several manuscripts it is possible to discern the hands of the same scribes. We may also suppose, even before studying their content, that certain works were composed at Khirbet Qumran. But beyond this we cannot go. The study of the archaeological remains of the Qumran area has shown that it was occupied by a group of individuals who practised agriculture and certain industries, and who lived under a community régime with special rules and rites. While we do not exclude the possibility that the people concerned could have sold the manuscripts which they copied for gain, we must recognize that those found in the caves, whether they had been copied on

---

[1] *Comptes Rendus de L'Académie des inscriptions et belles-lettres* (1953), 319; cf. (1955), 385.

[2] *Syria*, xxxv (1958), 2.

the spot or had come from elsewhere, were in the possession of the community and read by its members. They constituted its library and hence they can be used to determine the special interests of the group. The fact that the manuscripts were dispersed throughout the caves can be accounted for in various ways. It may be that these were texts which one particular member or small group of members within the community had at their disposal, and that they left them behind in the cave in which they had been living (Caves 5, 7 to 9). Alternatively they may have been stored or hidden, together with their crockery, in a cavity near their camping place (Caves 2, 3, 6). But more than 400 had been placed in Cave 4, and it is situated very close to Khirbet Qumran. It is here that the community library, normally kept together in the central buildings, was hastily hidden at the moment when the settlement was abandoned. A possible explanation of the important group of Cave 1 is that it may be part of this same library, but stored in a safe place more carefully, and further from the Khirbeh. Alternatively Cave 1 may have been the hiding-place chosen by one group, more numerous than the rest, which had its living quarters near this particular cave.

We have been dealing so far with the question of how the manuscripts came to be collected in the Qumran caves, the character of the collection itself, its undoubted antiquity, and finally the connection between the caves and the buildings. Attempts have been made, however, to explain these points by a different hypothesis, one that does not envisage a special religious community established in the area. According to K. H. Rengstorf,[1] the documents have nothing to do either with the Essenes or with any other sect. They comprise part of the library of the temple at Jerusalem which was stored in a safe place at the time of the Jewish Revolt. The interpretation of the inscribed Copper Scroll as a list of the temple treasures would fit in well with this hypothesis. The choice of the Qumran caves would have been no accident. The temple property included an

---

[1] K. H. Rengstorf, *Ḥirbet Qumran und die Bibliothek vom Toten Meer*, Studia Delitzschiana 5 (1960). A somewhat abridged English edition, without the large number of notes, has been published, *Ḥirbet Qumrân and the Problem of the Dead Sea Caves* (1963).

agricultural and industrial estate in the area, evidence of which is preserved in the ruins of Khirbet Qumran and Feshkha, and it is natural that this estate should have been managed by priestly personnel as the manuscripts state.[1] The presentation of this theory, which is personal to Rengstorf himself, is preceded by a critique of the 'Essene' theory in the form in which it has often been presented, and the author rightly emphasizes the weakness or ambiguity of certain lines of argument. But his own explanation entails great difficulties.[2] We are very ill-informed about what landed property the Second Temple may have possessed as the distant inheritor of the possessions of the kings. In any case it is doubtful whether it either had or retained such estates in so abandoned an area as Qumran, and this doubt changes into absolute disbelief when we remember that from about 600 to 150 B.C. the site remained deserted. On the other hand the proportions of the communal buildings of Qumran, the number of the caves made use of, and the great cemetery of more than a thousand tombs are out of proportion with the needs of the personnel attached to an estate of a few square kilometres. On the contrary, all these factors imply the existence of an organized community which made use of the buildings and caves and which was forced, at some particular point of time, to abandon the site but to leave its library behind there.

IV. THE DATE WHEN THE MANUSCRIPTS
WERE ABANDONED

The date of the abandonment can be determined. These manuscripts, belonging to the community which occupied Khirbet Qumran and the caves, could only have been deposited in the caves during the time when the community was at Qumran, i.e. between the second half of the second century B.C. and A.D. 68.[3]

---

[1] K. H. Rengstorf has returned to this point, 'Erwägungen zur Frage des Landbesitzes des zweiten Tempels in Judäa und seiner Verwaltung', *Bibel und Qumran . . .*, ed. S. Wagner (1968), 156–76.

[2] They have been pointed out in particular by H. Bardtke, *Theologische Literaturzeitung*, LXXXVII (1962), 820–3; *Theologische Rundschau*, XXXIII (1968), 101–5.

[3] Cf. pp. 3–41.

The point which concerns us here is when the manuscripts were deposited in the caves and not the date when they were copied, still less the date at which the works contained in them were composed. There are some works (all the biblical books) and some manuscripts (certain biblical manuscripts) which are earlier than the installation of the community at Qumran. But none of the works could have been composed, and none of the manuscripts either written, copied, or placed in the caves after June A.D. 68, the point at which the life of the community at Qumran was brought to an end.

It might be objected that some members of the community could have continued to live in or near the caves even after the buildings had been destroyed, or that they could have returned there to hide the manuscripts. But a military outpost had been set up at Khirbet Qumran and the caves—or at least some of them—were very close to the buildings. It is unlikely that any members of the community would either have remained in, or returned to the caves under the eyes of their enemies, the Roman soldiers.

It would be more reasonable to suppose that, after the Roman soldiers had departed, some members of the community or some Jews who had not been members of it came to Qumran and deposited the manuscripts there. In the buildings we have discovered traces of the ruins having been used by the rebels of the Second Jewish War in A.D. 132–5. They could have used the caves as well, and in fact two or three caves in the rock cliffs contained elements of pottery which seem a little later than the occupation of Qumran by the community. But these are not the caves where the manuscripts were found. A further point is that if the rebels entrenched themselves or hid themselves in a ruined building and, it may be, in some of the caves, they still did not re-establish any community life there. Finally, some documents, reliably dated to the Second Revolt, have been discovered in other areas in the Judaean Desert. They are different in type, in epigraphy, and in the biblical texts to which they bear witness. The manuscripts of Qumran precede them in date, and were certainly not deposited in the caves at the time of the Second Jewish War.

But could they not have been deposited at some point prior to this war, yet after the departure of the Roman soldiers—probably, therefore, at some point after A.D. 73?[1] It is highly improbable that any manuscripts would have been left in this way by members of the community. There is nothing to indicate either that the ruins were reoccupied or that community life was resumed at any point between these two dates. If we recognize that there is a connection between the manuscripts, the caves, and the buildings we must admit that at least some of the manuscripts—the majority—were laid in the caves during the period when the community was in residence, or abandoned there at the end of that period. On the other hand we cannot see any motive which would have prompted isolated members of the community to return to an area which their group had abandoned for the sole purpose of depositing some manuscripts in caves which were no longer in use. If they ever did return it would rather have been in order to retrieve the manuscripts which they had left behind when they quitted the settlement.

One single possibility remains before we have exhausted all the hypotheses. It is that at some period when the area was deserted certain manuscripts were hidden or left in the caves by unknown individuals, and that by chance these have been discovered together with the manuscripts of the community. The point would have to be proved in each individual instance by means of internal and external criticism of the manuscript itself, and by considering its situation in the cave in relation to the other documents. I can see only a single case to which such extraordinary circumstances might, with any likelihood, be held to apply, that namely of the inscribed Copper Scroll from Cave 3. From every point of view it is different from the generality of the manuscripts at Qumran. It is the only document engraved on metal, and the only text in Mishnaic Hebrew. In content it does not conform to any of the literary *genres* attested at Qumran. It consists of a catalogue of treasures which are allegedly hidden throughout Palestine. It was found in the outer part of the cave, resting against the rock wall a little to one side of the mass of broken pottery and inscribed fragments of skin and papyrus intermingled with the sherds. When he was preparing the edition of the text J. T. Milik initially dated it

[1] pp. 44–5.

before the end of the community occupation, about the middle of the first century A.D.[1] However, in the final stages of his editorial work[2] he modified his earlier conclusions and inclined to a rather later date, about A.D. 100. In this he was prompted by certain linguistic and palaeographic traits, and also by the fact that some of the imaginary treasures recorded in the scroll seemed to be located on the site of Khirbet Qumran, as though it were already in ruins. The arguments are not decisive but, as we shall explain, no serious objection to them arises from the archaeological evidence. The only point we would make here is that this exception, if it were indeed shown to be such, would serve to prove the rule: it would be easier to explain the unique character of this document, so foreign to the outlook and preoccupations of the community, if it emanated from some other source and had been deposited at a later stage. This would confirm our conclusion: none of the manuscripts belonging to the community is later than the ruin of Khirbet Qumran in A.D. 68.

V. THE ORGANIZATION AND LIFE OF THE COMMUNITY

Having thus established the connection between the manuscripts and the ruins, we may justifiably proceed to relate the evidence of the texts to that of the archaeological remains, to see how they agree, and how each throws light upon the other. Three points will be touched upon in turn: the organization of the community, its history, and finally its distinctive character. In this section and those which follow, we shall be making no attempt to examine *ex professo* questions which essentially belong to the study of the texts. Our concern will be merely to assemble those points on which archaeology can contribute towards the solution.

Archaeology has shown that a relatively numerous community lived in the settlements of Khirbet Qumran and Feshkha and in the caves or near caves in the vicinity. Having installed itself in

---

[1] In *Biblical Archaeologist*, XIX (1956), 62; *Dix ans de découvertes dans le Désert de Juda* (1957), 110; *Ten Years of Discovery in the Wilderness of Judaea* (1959), 95.
[2] 'Le Rouleau de cuivre de Qumrân (3Q 15)', *Revue biblique*, LXVI (1959), 321–57, and above all Discoveries in the Judaean Desert, III (1962), 199–302.

an area which was extremely poor, this group drew its sustenance from the products of stock-rearing, some types of cultivation, and certain industries. The archaeological evidence suggests to us that this group was a religious community. It was organized, disciplined, and observed special rites.

Now the manuscripts of Qumran include a *Rule of the Community*, several copies of which had been made. One of them, coming from the first cave, is in a remarkable state of preservation. The same scroll contained a *Rule of the Congregation*, slightly different in its spirit and precepts.[1] Again several manuscripts were found in the caves of a text which had already been known under the name of the *Damascus Document*. It had been discovered more than half a century earlier in the ancient Qaraite synagogue of Cairo in two copies from the tenth to the twelfth centuries A.D. It records the rule of a Jewish group which went to live in the 'land of Damascus' (we shall be returning to this expression), there to lead a way of life similar to that prescribed in the *Rule of the Community*. It would go beyond the limits of this book to study these three rules and the relationship which each bears to the others, and we shall confine ourselves simply to certain major features, for the most part taking the *Rule of the Community* as our basis.

The community here calls itself the Remnant of Israel, the True Israel, the New Covenant. Its members have separated themselves from Israel and its priesthood, which in their eyes has prevaricated. They have withdrawn to the desert and there lead a common life of work, prayer, and study of the sacred Law. Before anyone is admitted to the community he must first undergo a period of probation and a novitiate. The community is hierarchically organized with a priest and a supervisor or overseer at its head. It has a limited council and general assemblies. It holds reunions for the purpose of prayer and religious meals. All this is strikingly in agreement with the isolated position of the settlements at Khirbet Qumran and Feshkha in the desert, and the collective function of the major

---

[1] The 'Rule of the Congregation' is the text published by D. Barthélemy in Discoveries in the Judaean Desert, I, no. 28a. The 'Rule of the Community' is the work published by Millar Burrows under the title 'Manual of Discipline' in *The Dead Sea Scrolls of St. Mark's Monastery*, II, 2 (1951).

part of the buildings. On specific points of detail, the organization and rules prescribed here justify the term 'council chamber' which we have suggested for the room surrounded by a bench at loc. 4, and our proposed interpretation of the large room, loc. 77, as being at once an assembly room and a dining hall. We have concluded that religious meals were eaten there, the remains of which were ritually buried at various points in the Khirbeh. It is true that neither the *Rule of the Community* nor any other text from Qumran contains any allusion to this particular rite for the deposits of bones, and the absence of such allusions is regrettable. But there is no doubt that all these prescriptions of the Rule could be observed in the installations of Khirbet Qumran.

VI. HISTORY OF THE COMMUNITY

Some pieces of information on the history of the community are available to us in the *Damascus Document* and the biblical commentaries, in which the sacred texts are interpreted as predictions or foreshadowings of what has befallen the community. Unfortunately these indications are enigmatic. They avoid proper names and convey their message by means of veiled allusions. Hence the various stages in the community's history, the relevant dates, and still more the identity of the individuals who play a part in it, are the subject of lively discussion among the experts. According to the *Damascus Document* and the commentaries the founder of the group is the Teacher of Righteousness or the Righteous Teacher, a greatly revered individual who has profoundly influenced the organization and spirituality of the community, but who remains, so far as we are concerned, enveloped in mystery. He had an adversary, the Evil Priest or Wicked Priest, and on this figure the texts with which we are concerned are a little more explicit. Obviously the identity of the Teacher of Righteousness or the Evil Priest cannot be determined from the archaeological evidence. The answer to these questions can be arrived at only on the basis of an interpretation of the texts and by correlating them with the data of external history. But archaeology does provide a chronological

framework, and thereby prescribes certain limits for the possible hypotheses.

Let us recall the results of our inquiry. The community
installed itself at Qumran in the second half of the second
century B.C. It abandoned the site for a period of some thirty
years during the reign of Herod the Great, and definitively left
the area in A.D. 68.

It is certain that some relationship does exist between the
community of Qumran and the members of the New Covenant
for whom the *Damascus Document* was composed. In fact copies
of this document have been discovered in the caves, the vocabu-
lary and spirituality are similar, and above all the two groups
invoke the authority of the Teacher of Righteousness. But the
Damascus Document speaks of the 'Converts of Israel who went out
from the land of Judah and were exiled in the land of Damascus',
6: 5, cf. 4: 2–3. They are 'those who have entered the New
Covenant in the land of Damascus', 6: 19; 8: 21, cf. 19: 33–4.
Our first impulse is to take these texts in the literal sense, and to
understand them, as many authors do, to refer to an exodus of
travellers to Damascus. Here, then, is a very difficult problem,
which is also of concern to the archaeologist. If this exodus
involved the community as a whole it cannot have taken place
later than the end of the occupation at Qumran, for witnesses to
the *Damascus Document* have been found there. On the other hand
we cannot assign this sojourn at Damascus to a date prior to the
settlement at Qumran since at two points (19: 35–20: 1; 20: 14)
the *Damascus Document* refers to the death of the Teacher of
Righteousness who installed the community at Qumran.
Furthermore, the situation reflected in the *Damascus Document*
seems to be later than that envisaged in the *Rule of the Community*.
On these grounds one might think of placing this exodus during
the period of abandonment of Khirbet Qumran under the reign
of Herod.[1] But this solution is ruled out by certain considerations
of the internal evidence and by palaeography. One copy of the

---

[1] I had pointed out this possibility in *Revue biblique*, LXI (1954), 235–6,
though without actually committing myself to it. The hypothesis has been
upheld by C. T. Fritsch, 'Herod the Great and the Qumran Community',
Journal of Biblical Literature, LXXIV (1955), 173–81, and accepted by F. F.
Bruce, *Second Thoughts on the Dead Sea Scrolls* (1956), 108.

Damascus Document from Cave 4 is certainly earlier than the abandonment of Khirbet Qumran in 31 B.C.[1] The only remaining solution would be to admit that it was only one part of the community which left the 'land of Judah' to go to the 'land of Damascus'. This schism could have arisen right at the origin of the community, even before it settled at Khirbet Qumran. Alternatively, if it did take place after the settlement, it must have been fairly soon afterwards, for one of the manuscripts of the Damascus Document is contemporary with Period I*b*.[2] However, if the group did in fact lead an independent existence at Damascus, and whatever its relations may have been with the 'mother house' at Qumran, it is difficult to explain why so many manuscripts of the *Damascus Document* should have been found in the caves: seven copies in Cave 4, one in Cave 5, one in Cave 6—almost as many, in other words, as of the *Rule of the Community* (twelve manuscripts), and almost as many as the most frequently read books of the bible, Isaiah, the Psalms, and the Minor Prophets, and more than any of the books of the Pentateuch except Deuteronomy. The *Damascus Document* is certainly at home at Qumran.

In the light of this one is tempted to agree with those authors who interpret the 'land of Damascus' as a symbolic name for the Qumran area.[3] The name would have been borrowed from Amos 5: 26–7. In the *Damascus Document* 7: 14–21 this passage is quoted in a form which makes Damascus a place of exile, and in the free commentary which follows this place of exile becomes a refuge where the true faithful are saved from the anger of God. Here we recognize the theology of the deportation in Jeremiah. The exiles of Judah represent that part of the people which remained faithful, and which Yahweh protects, Jer. 24: 5–7; 29. The exiles are the true Remnant of Israel, Jer. 31: 2–7, as they are for Ezekiel, 11: 13–16, and it is with them that Yahweh sealed a new covenant, Ezek. 11: 17–20; 36: 24–8; Jer. 31: 31–4. At the same time the 'New Covenant' as applied to the group of

[1] Cf. F. M. Cross, *The Ancient Library of Qumran* . . ., 2nd edn. (1961), 81–3; J. T. Milik, *Ten Years of Discovery* . . ., 91 n. 2.

[2] This is the view taken by J. T. Milik, *Dix ans de découvertes* . . ., 59 f.; *Ten Years of Discovery* . . ., 90.

[3] The most recent of these authors is A. Jaubert, 'Le pays de Damas', *Revue biblique*, LXV (1958), 214–48; F. M. Cross, *loc. cit.*

the 'land of Damascus' finds its explanation in this spirituality. Apart from the use of the actual name Damascus, we encounter the same spirituality in the texts of the Qumran community. The members 'enter into the Covenant', and the renewal of the Covenant is celebrated each year, *Rule of the Community*, 1: 16–2: 19. The *Habakkuk Commentary* speaks of the New Covenant, 2: 3. The same commentary states that the Teacher of Righteousness was persecuted by the Wicked Priest 'in his place of exile', 11: 6. The *Rule for the War*, 1: 2, calls the community 'the deportation of the desert'.

If we assume that the 'land of Damascus' is the Qumran area, we then have to explain why it is necessary to 'go out from the land of Judah' in order to arrive there. R. North has attempted to find the solution in the sphere of historical geography. He suggests that in the first century B.C. the Nabataeans were in control of the north-west shore of the Dead Sea and, since at that time they were in possession of Damascus, the Qumran area could be considered as part of the 'land of Damascus' and so as lying outside the 'land of Judah'.[1] But the assumption that Nabataean power was extended to the Qumran area is a conjecture unsupported by any text or any evidence from archaeology,[2] and the designation of the Nabataean kingdom as the 'land of Damascus' would be unprecedented. Our proper course is rather to forget political frontiers and to recognize that the 'land of Judah' has a symbolic significance similar to that which is accepted for the 'land of Damascus'. The prophetic texts quoted above draw a contrast between the exiles who will be saved, and the inhabitants of Jerusalem and Judah who will be punished, Jer. 24: 8–10; 29: 16–19. In the *Damascus Document* itself the House of Judah is declared to be fallen, 4: 11, the princes of Judah are condemned as unfaithful, 8: 1–13; 19: 15–22. On this showing the 'land of Judah' designates the prince-priest class of Jerusalem and its adherents, and it is from these that the 'exiles' of Damascus-Qumran have separated themselves.

[1] R. North, 'The Damascus of Qumran Geography', *Palestine Exploration Quarterly* (1955), 34–48.

[2] Only four Nabataean coins of the first century A.D. have been recovered at Khirbet Qumran in contrast to some hundreds of coins of the Jewish princes and procurators.

However, between the *Damascus Document* and the *Rule of the Community* certain differences do exist which must not be underestimated.[1] They relate particularly to the social structure, and exclude the possibility that the two rules would have been followed at the same time by the same group. Furthermore, these differences are such that they cannot be explained by any process of evolution in the interior discipline of the community. If 'Damascus' is a symbolic name for Qumran it follows that we must admit that several groups existed side by side at Qumran who agreed on essentials but did not have an organization or way of life that were identical. Possibly this would also apply to the *Rule of the Congregation*. The findings of archaeology may perhaps lend some support to this hypothesis. The caves in the rock cliffs contained provision jars and domestic crockery, pots, bowls, and juglets. This suggests that the individuals or groups living in the caves or near them followed a rule of life that was partly independent. The *Damascus Document* sets forth the rule for the *maḥanôt*, the 'camps' established in the 'land of Damascus', 12: 22–3; 13: 7, 20 etc., and it is apparent that although these camps were subject to a single common leader, 14: 8–9, they possessed a certain autonomy. The 'camps' could have been the huts and tents set up at the foot of the rock cliffs of Qumran. On the other hand, in contrast to the *Rule of the Community*, the *Damascus Document* (7: 6–7; 19: 2–3), as also the *Rule of the Congregation*, provides for the members being able to marry and have children. This might account for the women and children buried in the secondary cemeteries.

Two of the most controversial points in the history of the group are the dating and identification of the Teacher of Righteousness and his adversary, the Wicked Priest. There can be no question of entering into this discussion here, in which the relevant passages are interpreted in opposite senses. Our sole concern will be to apply the evidence of archaeology to the problem. It is generally conceded that the Teacher of Righteousness was the founder, or at least the organizer of the community, that he had cut himself off from Judaism in its official forms, and had led his adherents into the desert. It is further conceded that

[1] Cf. L. Rost, 'Zur Struktur der Gemeinde des Neuen Bundes im Lande Damascus', *Vetus Testamentum*, IX (1959), 393–8.

his opponent, the Wicked Priest, is one of the line of high priests who succeeded one another in the leadership of the priestly class at Jerusalem. The strife between the two individuals began with the schism and continued after it. The most explicit reference is to an episode mentioned in the *Habakkuk Commentary*, 11: 4–8: 'Its meaning concerns the Wicked Priest who persecuted the Teacher of Righteousness, trying in angry fury to devour him in the abode of his exile. At the time of the Feast of Rest, the Day of Atonement, he appeared before them to swallow them up and to cause them to stumble on the Day of Fasting, their sabbath of rest.' This attack upon the Teacher of Righteousness and his faithful ones (notice the plural in the second phrase) implies that the community had already been constituted as a separate body.[1] The Teacher of Righteousness and his adherents are already in 'exile', and the most natural conclusion is that the place of exile is Qumran, since we do not know of any other place where the community lived outside Jerusalem prior to their installation at Qumran. It is the same Wicked Priest who, by his conduct, has been the cause of the secession and who has come to Qumran with evil intent. He is the high priest in the course of whose pontificate the community was installed at Qumran. Hence although the archaeological evidence makes an important contribution, it is, as we have seen, inconclusive.[2] The first installation, Period I*a*, is certainly earlier than Alexander Jannaeus (103–76 B.C.). It seems, therefore, that archaeology rules out any attempt to identify the Wicked Priest with Alexander Jannaeus or his successor Hyrcanus II (76–40 B.C.), though a certain number of authors consider that he might be one or the other of these figures. Period I*a* may possibly have begun under John Hyrcanus, 134–104 B.C., or one of his immediate predecessors, his father Simon, 143–134 B.C., or his uncle Jonathan, the high priest from 152 to 143 B.C. Of these three candidates for the title of the Wicked Priest John Hyrcanus can first be set aside since his career and activities do not correspond to what the documents tell us about the Wicked Priest. There remain Simon and

---

[1] And with a special calendar of its own. The Day of Atonement observed by the community differs from that of the official Judaism, a day on which the high priest would not have left Jerusalem.

[2] Cf. p. 5.

Jonathan. The indications in the documents correspond well with what we know of the latter, and in fact G. Vermès and J. T. Milik have put forward sound arguments for identifying him with the Wicked Priest.[1] F. M. Cross, however, has suggested, on no less solid grounds, that Simon is the figure referred to.[2] The findings of archaeology suggest that Period Ia was of brief duration, and this makes it inadvisable to go back much earlier than the reign of John Hyrcanus and favours the candidacy of Simon rather than Jonathan. But it cannot supply any positive arguments to support this solution, and its findings on the question are not decisive.

Some authors, however, assign the career of the Teacher of Righteousness, his conflict with the Wicked Priest, and the composition of at least some of the works discovered at Qumran, to a much later period. According to them the historical background would have been that of the First Jewish War. This thesis has been upheld by C. Roth and G. R. Driver.[3] We shall concentrate first on the arguments put forward by C. Roth.[4]

[1] G. Vermès, *Discovery in the Judaean Desert* (1956), 91–4; J. T. Milik, *Ten Years of Discovery* . . ., 84–7. The positions adopted by these authors have been followed to a large extent by P. Winter, 'The Wicked Priest', *Hibbert Journal*, LVIII (1959), 53–60; G. Jeremias, *Der Lehrer der Gerechtigkeit* (1963), 36–78; M. Hengel, *Judentum und Hellenismus* (1969), 407–10.

[2] F. M. Cross, *The Ancient Library* . . ., 2nd edn., 134–53.

[3] The theory had already been put forward in general outline in connection with the *Habakkuk Commentary* by H. Del Medico, *Deux Manuscrits de la Mer Morte* (1951); cf. *idem, L'Énigme des manuscrits de la Mer Morte* (1957), 182–7.

[4] Especially the following: *The Historical Background of the Dead Sea Scrolls*, (1958). The work was re-edited in 1965 under the title *The Dead Sea Scrolls. A New Historical Approach*. In spite of this change of title the new volume is simply a reproduction of the 1958 version, the only additions being a short introduction taken from an article of the *Commentary* of 1964 and three supplementary appendices: 'H. The Era of the Habakkuk Commentary', which had previously appeared in *Vetus Testamentum*, XI (1961), 'I. The Zealots—A Jewish Sect', which had appeared in *Judaism*, VIII (1959). The only completely new feature is Appendix J, two pages in which the principal characters in the non-biblical texts of Qumran are enumerated and described. To this the following articles may be added: 'The Jewish Revolt against the Romans (66–73) in the Light of the Dead Sea Scrolls', *Palestine Exploration Quarterly* (1958), 104–21; 'The Zealots in the War of 66–73', *Journal of Semitic Studies*, IV (1959), 332–55; 'Why the Qumran Sect Cannot have been Essenes', *Revue de Qumran*, I, 3 (Feb. 1959), 417–22; 'The Zealots and Qumran: the Basic Issue', *Revue de Qumran*, II, 1 (Nov. 1959), 81–4; 'Were

Our concern with them is all the greater in view of the fact that this author alleges that his conclusions have been brought into conformity with those of archaeology. According to him the two occupations of Khirbet Qumran in Periods I*b* and II were different in character. In Period I*b* it was probably the Essenes who were in occupation, while in Period II it was the Zealots. Following the death of Herod in 4 B.C. Judas the Galilean stirred up a revolt, and after meeting with a reverse may have fled with his adherents to Damascus while he organized the Zealot party as the 'New Covenant in the land of Damascus'. After a certain time the group returned to Judaea and installed itself in the buildings at Khirbet Qumran, which had been abandoned ever since 31 B.C. Shortly after the deposition of Herod Archelaus in A.D. 6 Judas was killed by the Romans, and forty years later his two sons underwent the same fate. Their brother Menahem then took over the leadership of the movement. When the insurrection against Rome broke out in A.D. 66 Menahem and his adherents left Khirbet Qumran for Masada, where they plundered the armoury. They advanced upon Jerusalem and attached themselves to the less resolute group already engaged there in combat against the Romans. The city was liberated almost in its entirety, but then a conflict arose between Menahem, who was intoxicated by his victory, and the captain of the temple, Eleazar ben Hanania, who had directed the earlier hostilities against the Romans. Menahem presented himself at the temple in royal attire. Eleazar ben Hanania stirred the people up against him and drove him out together with his followers. One individual, an associate of Menahem named Absalom, was killed. Menahem himself took refuge on the Ophel, where he was captured, tortured, and put to death in the autumn of 66. His kinsman, Eleazar ben Jair, succeeded in escaping with a group of loyal followers to Masada. Throughout all this time Khirbet Qumran remained in the hands of the Zealots, who devoted themselves energetically to the work of copying the propagandist literature of the party. In A.D. 73 Masada fell at

the Qumran Sectaries Essenes? A Re-examination of some Evidences', *Journal of Theological Studies*, N.S. x (1959), 87–93; 'Qumrân and Masada: A Final Clarification Regarding the Dead Sea Sect', *Revue de Qumran*, v, 1 (October 1964), 81–8.

the hands of the Romans, and its defendants, Eleazar ben Jair among them, committed suicide. C. Roth has reconstructed this new history of the Zealots by combining the data of Josephus with the references in the Qumran documents. He concedes that not all the points in his reconstruction are equally assured or even have the same degree of probability. But he asserts that the following conclusions at least are established: the occupants of Khirbet Qumran in the first century A.D. were Zealots. The Teacher of Righteousness was Menahem or his nephew(?), Eleazar ben Jair. The House of Absalom, which the Habakkuk Commentary reproaches with not having come to the aid of the Teacher of Righteousness, was the party of that Absalom who was killed at Jerusalem. The Wicked Priest was Eleazar ben Hanania. The Qumran documents relating to the Teacher of Righteousness and his conflict with the Wicked Priest were composed after A.D. 66.

Other critics, notably A. Dupont-Sommer and H. H. Rowley, have pointed out the improbabilities of this reconstruction and the weakness of the arguments. The lack of historical method in C. Roth's presentation has been most severely criticized by Morton Smith.[1] The only point on which I shall dwell here is the one which C. Roth presents as his basic and, as he says, irrefutable, argument.[2] If the occupants of Qumran were not Zealots we are forced to admit that in A.D. 67/68 there were two politico-religious communities living a few miles distant from one another on the shores of the Dead Sea who (a) began a new phase in their existence in or about the year A.D. 6, (b) were fanatically opposed both to the priestly authorities at Jerusalem and to the Romans, (c) venerated the personal qualities of a teacher who had had a certain Absalom as his close associate, (d) invoked the authority of a Teacher who had been assailed by a 'Wicked' Priest on or about the Day of Atonement.

It would be absurd, Roth argues, to attribute such a coincidence, extending down to the very details, to mere chance. But is there really any coincidence here? The distance between Masada and Khirbet Qumran is not 'a few miles' but almost

[1] Morton Smith, 'Zealots and Sicarii, their Origins and Relation', *Harvard Theological Review*, LXIV (1971), 1–19, especially 6–10.
[2] Most recently, *Revue de Qumran*, II, 1 (Nov. 1959), 81.

fifty kilometres of a terrain which can be crossed only with difficulty.[1] The reoccupation of Khirbet Qumran in Period II was accomplished at latest in the year 1 B.C./A.D. 1.[2] Yet according to Roth the occupation of Khirbet Qumran by the Zealots would have taken place a little after A.D. 6.[3] He refuses to concede that the occupiers of Period II belonged to the same group which had left Qumran in 31 B.C. Yet the identity between them is assured by the fact that a plan adapted to a particular way of life was preserved, that the main features were left to function as they had before, and that the same industries were retained (the potter's workshop was in use at both periods and maintained the same ceramic tradition). But the clearest proof of all is, perhaps, the evidence that so special a rite as the burying of the bones was observed at both periods.[4] To designate both groups as 'politico-religious' is to assimilate them to one another unduly. According to its literature the community of Qumran was pre-eminently a religious group, and was opposed, pre-eminently, to the official Judaism. The party of the Zealots, on the other hand, was, according to all that Josephus tells us of it, first and foremost a nationalist party and was opposed, first and foremost, to the Romans. The community of Qumran had received its statutes and drawn its inspiration from a Teacher of Righteousness whom it venerated. The Zealots were organized by Judas the Galilean whom Josephus calls a 'sophist'. Even if this word can signify 'teacher', the title is never given to Eleazar ben Jair, yet according to Roth it is either he or his kinsman Menahem who is the Teacher of Righteousness. In no passage are either Judas, Menahem, or Eleazar credited with a teaching or an influence comparable to those of the Teacher of Righteousness of Qumran. It is not even stated in any passage that any one of these three individuals was

[1] It cannot be objected that the Qumran community extended as far as 'Ain Feshkha (3 km. to the south) and that the Zealots of Masada were in control of En-Gedi. In *Bell.* IV. vii. 402–5, Josephus states merely that the 'brigands' of Masada made a raid upon En-Gedi at the time of the Passover of 68, and took the plunder from it to Masada.

[2] Cf. pp. 33–6.

[3] This seems to be his most recent position, *Palestine Exploration Quarterly*, (1958), 107 n. 1.

[4] Cf. pp. 12–14.

venerated by the Zealots. The Qumran documents reproach the 'House of Absalom' with not having come to the support of the Teacher of Righteousness. But the Absalom spoken of by Josephus did support Menahem to the point of dying with him, and the Jewish historian speaks neither of his adherents (if he had any) nor of their attitude with regard to Menahem.[1] According to the Qumran texts the Wicked Priest's attack upon the Teacher of Righteousness took place on the Day of Atonement. According to Josephus the pursuit and death of Menahem is to be assigned to the month of Gorpieus (which the best commentators on Josephus regard as equivalent to Elul and not to Tishri), and his account contains no allusion to the Day of Atonement. There is no need to be astonished at 'coincidences' which do not exist.

Roth then had the idea that the excavations of Masada contributed a striking confirmation of his theory. In fact a scroll-fragment was discovered there[2] deriving from a work other parts of which have been found at Qumran, and which contains a list of prescriptions for the chants used at the Sabbath sacrifice.[3] This document is, in fact, representative of the outlook and way of life of Qumran, and is equally well attested there. But in Roth's view its presence at Masada constitutes irrefutable proof of the identity of the two communities. In both cases they are 'Zealots/Sicarii'.[4] Yet the suggestion put forward by Y. Yadin as soon as the discovery was made has remained the most natural and satisfying explanation of how this fragment from a Qumran writing should have been present at Masada: it had been carried there by some refugees who attached themselves to the

[1] The only information which Josephus supplies on this Absalom is contained in a single phrase (following his mention of the death of Menahem): 'His lieutenants underwent the same fate, as also did Absalom, the most famous instrument of his tyranny', Bell. II. xvi. 448.

[2] Y. Yadin, Masada. First Season of Excavations, 1963–1964 (1965), 105–8. Idem, Masada (1966), 172–4.

[3] J. Strugnell, 'The Angelic Liturgy at Qumrân—4Q Serek širôt 'ôlat haššabât', Supplements to Vetus Testamentum VII, Congress Volume. Oxford 1959 (1960), 318–45.

[4] C. Roth, 'Qumran and Masada: A Final Clarification regarding the Dead Sea Sect', Revue de Qumran, v, 1 (Oct. 1964), 81–7. The problem is further complicated by that confusion between the Zealots and the Sicarii which goes back to Josephus, and from which even the most recent publications continue to suffer. Cf. Morton Smith, Harvard Theological Review, LXIV (1971), 1–19.

defendants of Masada after the ruin of Qumran in June 68.[1]
We were already aware that the Essenes took part in the revolt.
Josephus refers to a certain John the Essene who had been
governor of the regions of Thimna, Lydda, Joppa, and Emmaus
in 66–7 before dying at the time of the ill-fated attack upon
Ashkelon.[2] We do not know how many Essenes took part in the
revolt, but we do know, at least from the archaeological evidence,
that one part of the Qumran community defended itself against
the Roman attackers to the bitter end.[3]

The evidence of palaeography is equally hostile to Roth's
theory. It is true that he refuses to take it into account, but he
admits that it can supply an approximate date to within about
one generation.[4] This is sufficient for us. If conscientious palaeographers assign the copying of the earliest examples of the *Rule
of the Community* and the *Damascus Document* to the first half of the
first century B.C. (the actual composition is still earlier), these
documents could not have been written for a group which was
brought into being only at the beginning of the first century A.D.

The archaeological evidence is at least as hostile to Roth's
theory. As we are about to explain, the occupation of Period II
of Khirbet Qumran in the first century B.C. represents a prolongation, after an interruption, of Period I*b*, and the period to
which it belongs was one in which the Zealots had not yet come
into being. We have already shown at an earlier stage[5] that the
end of Period II and the ruin of Khirbet Qumran took place in
June A.D. 68. If the Teacher of Righteousness is Menahem, who
died in the autumn of 66, the composing and copying of all the
works alluding to the persecution and death of the Teacher of
Righteousness, and the depositing of them in the caves, would
have had to be achieved within a space of less than two years.
This is extremely difficult. If the Teacher of Righteousness is
Eleazar ben Jair, who died in 73, it is impossible, or rather we

---

[1] Y. Yadin, *Masada*, 174.

[2] *Bell.* II. xx. 567; III. ii. 11 and 19.

[3] Cf. above pp. 36 f.

[4] The condemnation is pronounced 'once and for all', and in capital letters
in *Revue de Qumran*, II, 1 (Nov. 1959), 84. Yet on the same page we read that
palaeography can serve to fix the approximate date of these documents
'within a generation or so'.

[5] pp. 36–41.

would have to seek refuge in the hypothesis that certain documents written after the ruin of Khirbet Qumran were added to those deposited in the caves.[1] We have explained how improbable this is.[2]

Roth's small book is on quite a different scale from the major work by G. R. Driver, published some years later.[3] In this work one of the best Semitic scholars of our time, who has taken a lively interest in the Dead Sea Scrolls from the first, argues his thesis at length and in detail. Like Roth,[4] Driver considers that the historical background to the scrolls is the war against Rome of A.D. 66–73. They derive from the group known as the 'Men of the Covenant', and Driver calls them the 'Covenanters'. The movement they represent goes back to the schism which arose among the adherents of the Zadokite dynasty after the deposition or death of Onias III (170 B.C.). Some of them accepted the new situation and became the Sadducees of the New Testament. Others fled to Egypt with Onias IV. Some of these rebels in turn may have taken refuge at that time in the Judaean Desert (Periods I*a* and I*b* of Qumran?). After Pompey's intervention the Egyptian group returned to Jerusalem, and notable among them was the priest Boethus, who founded the party of the Boethusians. But after Boethus had become involved with Herod his group of followers rejected him and transferred their allegiance to Judas the Galilean who, together with Saddok, founded the Zealot party, the 'fourth philosophy' of Josephus. After the execution of Judas by the Romans in A.D. 6 the Zealots installed themselves at Qumran (Period II), becoming the

---

[1] The course adopted by Roth in *Palestine Exploration Quarterly* (1958), 120 n. 1. In the same note the author states that his reconstruction is fully in accord with the conclusions of archaeology 'except in one minor point': the most recent Jewish coins from 68 prove merely that 'the occupation ended about, not in, the year 68'. This would be true if it were not for the fact that some Roman coins, the earliest of which belong to 67/68, had not been found in the level of reconstruction, and if this date did not coincide with the arrival of the Roman troops in the vicinity of Qumran, cf. pp. 39–41. This is not 'a minor point', for it calls Roth's entire theory in question.

[2] pp. 106–9.

[3] G. R. Driver, *The Judaean Scrolls. The Problem and a Solution* (1965).

[4] The agreement between them is no accident. G. R. Driver and C. Roth had planned a joint publication, but Roth published the results of their work first and independently, without mentioning Driver's name.

'Covenanters'. Alternatively, if a group of Zadokite-Covenanters had already been in residence at Qumran in the second to the first centuries B.C., the Zealots amalgamated themselves with these. It can be regarded as reasonably certain that at the time of the Jewish War the Covenanters of Qumran were identical with the Zadokite-Boethusian-Zealot-Sicarii party. The references in the documents are to be explained by the history of the Zealots, who took an active part in the revolt of 66–73. The Wicked Priest is Eleazar, the captain of the temple. The Teacher of Righteousness is Menahem. The 'House of Absalom' is a reference to that Absalom who was Menahem's lieutenant. The 'House of Judah' designates the group which fled with Eleazar, the son of Jair, a descendant of Judas the Galilean, and which held out against the Romans at Masada up to the year 73. In accordance with this theory the chief writings are classified and dated as follows: the *Manual of Discipline* between A.D. 46–8 and 66; the *Copper Scroll*, 66–8; the *Habakkuk Commentary*, between 70 and 73; the *Hymns* between 73 and 81(?); the *War Scroll* during the reign of Domitian, 81–96, and perhaps in 85; the *Damascus Document* between 106 and 115.

G. R. Driver's study has met with the respect due to its author, and the scientific knowledge which he has brought to bear has been much admired.[1] However, the very critics who have praised these qualities in it have hesitated to accept his historical conclusions, or have even explicitly rejected them. In particular he has been criticized for not taking sufficiently into account the archaeological evidence and the conclusions which I have drawn from it in order to establish the history of the Qumran community and the date of the manuscripts. Hence I found myself faced with a task which I would gladly have avoided: that of showing how G. R. Driver's historical conclusions are incompatible with the most solidly established of the archaeological data.[2] He has replied to my criticisms in two articles in which

---

[1] I shall confine myself to the following references: M. Black, 'The Judaean Scrolls. i. The Scrolls and the New Testament', *New Testament Studies*, XIII (1966–7), 81–9; R. Le Déaut, 'Qumrân: une synthèse et une solution', *Biblica*, XLVII (1966), 445–56; H. H. Rowley, *Journal of Theological Studies*, N.S. XVII (1966), 422–6; H. Bardtke, *Theologische Rundschau*, XXXIII (1968), 105–19; id. *Theologische Literaturzeitung*, XCV (1970), cols. 7–9.

[2] R. de Vaux, 'Esséniens ou zélotes? A propos d'un livre récent', *Revue*

he attempts to dispel the 'myths' which have allegedly accumulated about Qumran.[1] In his most recent study he concludes that having re-read all the texts and taken due consideration of the criticisms which have been made to him, he has not found any reason for changing his opinion.

For my part I am compelled to say that his replies have failed to satisfy me, and that having read all that has been published since the first edition of this book, it serves merely to confirm my essential conclusions with regard to the date of the manuscripts. The dates which I have proposed for the pottery from the caves and from the buildings of Qumran at different periods have been accepted by all archaeologists and have been found to agree with the discoveries made at other sites.[2] In particular they have been confirmed by the excavations at Masada. Here the class of pottery which is certainly Herodian is well represented, and, while no counterparts to it have been found at Qumran, it does fit into the gap which I have recognized between the pottery of Periods I*b* and II, and which precisely covers the reign of Herod.[3] Those manuscripts discovered at Masada which are similar to the Qumran documents are certainly earlier than A.D. 73. It is true that Driver turns this argument in his own favour. He remarks that apart from the biblical texts fragments have been found at Masada of the *Book of Jubilees*, the antiquity of which is recognized, and also of the *Chants for the Sabbath Sacrifice* which, supposing that it is a Qumran writing, could have been written at a fairly early stage. But, Driver continues, nothing has been found of the major texts, the *Manual of Discipline*, the *Habakkuk Commentary*, the *Hymns*, the *War Scroll*, etc. Is not this because in A.D. 73 none of these writings had yet been composed?[4] But this line of argument presupposes that the communities of Qumran and Masada were identical and had the same literature. And

biblique, LXXIII (1966), 212–35; 'The Judaean Scrolls. ii. Essenes or Zelotes', *New Testament Studies*, XIII (1966–7), 89–104.

[1] G. R. Driver, 'Myths of Qumran', *Annual of Leeds University Oriental Society, VI, 1966–1968. Dead Sea Scrolls Studies* (1969), 23–48, especially 23–40; 'Mythology of Qumran', *Jewish Quarterly Review*, N.S. LXI (1970–1), 241–81, especially 241–50.

[2] P. Lapp, *Palestine Ceramic Chronology 200 B.C.–A.D. 70* (1961).

[3] Cf. Y. Yadin, 'Qumran and Masada', *Yediot*, XXX (1966), 117–27 (in Hebrew).

[4] *Jewish Quarterly Review*, art. cit., 242–3.

this is precisely the point upon which the whole question turns. I maintain that the buildings of Qumran were destroyed in June A.D. 68 by the Romans, who left a military outpost there for some years afterwards.[1] Here again the excavations at Masada have provided confirmation of the hypothesis. Numerous coins have been found there from all the years of the revolt down to the fourth and fifth. At Qumran, on the other hand, the latest Jewish coins discovered are from the third year, and not a single one has been discovered from the fourth or fifth. The only coins found at Qumran after this third year are Roman ones. Now this evidence makes it impossible to admit Driver's hypothesis, namely that a Jewish garrison dependent on Masada was stationed at Qumran and continued there after 68.

The destruction which took place in June 68 marks the end of the Jewish occupation at Qumran. The utilization of the caves is contemporary with the occupation of the buildings, as is proved by the identical pottery found in both, and it came to an end at the same time. The manuscripts derive from the Jewish community which occupied the buildings, and it cannot be proved (we have made an exception for the Copper Scroll, which is a very special case) that the manuscripts were brought into the caves at a later time. It follows that the date of the destruction also marks the point when the manuscripts were deposited or abandoned in the caves. None of them can be later than A.D. 68. Every hypothesis which places either the composition or the copying of the manuscripts after this date is ruled out by the archaeological evidence.

VII. THE AFFILIATION OF THE COMMUNITY

We shall now show that the archaeological evidence—to say nothing of the documents—prevents us from regarding the people of Qumran as Zealots. The same arguments rule out still more decisively the theory of J. L. Teicher, who interprets them as Judaeo-Christians.[2] Josephus distinguishes three main orders

[1] I have already set forth the arguments demonstrating this point above, pp. 36–41, 106–9, and in *Revue biblique*, LXXIII (1966), 232–5, and I will not repeat the arguments here.

[2] J. L. Teicher's thesis has been expounded chiefly in a series of articles in the *Journal of Jewish Studies*, II–IV (1951–4), and subsequently in 'The

or parties within Judaism, the Sadducees, Pharisees, and Essenes, and each of these in turn has had its advocates. Now archaeology does not exclude any of them from the outset, since all three were in existence during the time when the community was living at Qumran. But there are varying degrees of probability. The only point in favour of the connection with the Sadducees proposed by R. North[1] is the title of 'Sons of Zadok', frequently used in the Qumran writings, and the predominant role accorded by these to the priests. But their declared hostility to the Jerusalem priesthood makes it impossible to regard the people of Qumran as Sadducees. At most it might be said that they had separated themselves from them. But if this was the case, then it was only after the separation that they had any history of their own, and it is illusory to speak of a common origin. Stronger arguments have been put forward by C. Rabin[2] in defence of the theory that the Qumran community was Pharisaic in character. Rabin believes that this community continued the Pharisaic *ḥaburah* of the first century B.C., and that despite a considerable degree of evolution it represents Pharisaism in its primitive form more faithfully than the rabbinical schools of the first to the second centuries A.D. According to this author the most probable point at which the Qumran group would have come into conflict with the general movement of Pharisaism would have been after the ruin of Jerusalem. But in view of the date supplied by archaeology he would allow that the secession might have taken place as early as the first half of the first century A.D.[3] This reluctant concession is still not sufficient, for the community of Qumran was in existence as an autonomous entity at least from the first century B.C. onwards. Furthermore, this thesis, though learnedly argued, underestimates the differences between the Qumran community and

Essenes', *Studia Patristica*, I i, Texte und Untersuchungen 63 (1957), 540–5. Finally in *Antiquity*, XXXVII (1963), 30, Teicher announced that he was preparing a book in which he would show that the buildings of Qumran were originally a Christian sanctuary which was destroyed at the beginning of the fourth century, and subsequently reconstructed as a Byzantine monastery. The book has not appeared and the hypothesis does not merit any further consideration.

[1] R. North, 'The Qumrân "Sadducees"', *Catholic Biblical Quarterly*, XVII (1955), 44–68.

[2] C. Rabin, *Qumran Studies* (1957).　　　　[3] *loc. cit.* viii and 66.

Pharisaism in its most ancient form. Both the archaeological evidence and the texts show that the community had a far more developed and stable organization than the *ḥaburah* of the Pharisees. Furthermore, it was a group in which the priests held a predominant role, whereas Pharisaism was primarily a lay movement. Finally it followed a religious calendar which was different from that of the Pharisees, and this special characteristic is no late or secondary accretion. The adoption of a special calendar is an essential trait of the community, and was one of the causes—perhaps the main one—for its separation from official Judaism.

The prevailing opinion is that this community was related more or less closely to the Essenes. Clearly archaeology cannot prove that the people of Qumran were Essenes or were related to them. That is a question of doctrine, and the answer to it is to be sought from the texts rather than from the ruins. But in the writings of Qumran points of contact with, or resemblance to the beliefs and customs of, the Essenes have been brought to light. This being the case, we are justified in putting the question to the archaeologists whether the evidence in their field contradicts or corroborates this *rapprochement*. As one would expect, the answer is inconclusive.

The ancient sources of our knowledge of the Essenes, namely Philo, Pliny the Elder, and Josephus, say that they abstain from marriage. Pliny and Philo (the latter in his *Apologia pro Judaeis* quoted by Eusebius) are categorical on this point. Josephus simply says that they 'disdained' marriage, and adds that one of their groups allowed it. The witness of the writings of Qumran is ambiguous: the *Rule of the Community* presupposes that the members are celibate, but the *Rule of the Congregation* speaks of women and children, and the *Damascus Document* speaks of marriage. In the main cemetery and the secondary ones[1] we have marked down more than 1,200 tombs. Of these we have opened 43, and this number is quite inadequate to establish any valid statistical evidence. However, it does at least permit us to state certain specific findings: in the main cemetery, which was well laid out on the plateau of Qumran itself, we excavated 31 tombs, and among these there is only one which is certainly that

[1] Cf. pp. 45–8, 57–8.

of a woman. It is in a position apart from the general alignment, and is of a different type from the rest.[1] Six other tombs of women and four of children have been identified, but they are situated in the extensions to the main cemetery or in the two secondary ones. This may indicate that the women were not members of the community, or at any rate not in the same sense as the men buried in the main cemetery. It may also signify that a development had taken place in the discipline of the community. The rule of celibacy may have been relaxed, and marriage may have become lawful. This would explain why the tombs of women are located in what seem to be extensions to the main cemetery. Finally it may signify that there were different groups within the community,[2] a main group which would have renounced marriage (the central cemetery, in accordance with the *Rule of the Community*, Pliny, Philo, and the general rule as described in Josephus' account), and one or several groups which allowed it (the cemeteries annexed to the main one, in accordance with the *Rule of the Congregation*, the *Damascus Document*, and the particular case recorded by Josephus). Clearly the women's tombs do not strengthen the argument that the community was related to the Essenes, but they do not rule it out either.

Pliny says that the Essenes lived 'without money'. Philo tells us that they held all their possessions in common and delivered their earnings into the hands of a steward, while Josephus declares that on entering the sect they made over their fortunes to the community and had only a single patrimony in common administered by men of trust. These passages show that individual poverty was obligatory upon the members, but do not exclude the possibility that the community may have possessed goods. On the contrary they presuppose it. We found some hundreds of coins (almost all of bronze) in the buildings used for the community services or as living quarters for the administrators of the group. We did not find a single coin in the thirty or more caves which were used as living quarters, storage-places, or hiding-places by the members of the group. This might correspond to what the ancient authors tell us concerning the Essenes,

---

[1] This is Tomb 7, *Revue biblique*, LX (1953), 102–3.
[2] As we have already indicated on p. 115.

but on this point the Qumran documents themselves raise a difficulty. Their position with regard to individual poverty is equivocal. The *Rule of the Community* prescribes that personal possessions should be put into a common fund, yet in another passage it makes it obligatory for the individual to reimburse the community for any damage or loss incurred through him. This latter point is difficult to explain if the members did not have personal resources at their disposal. The *Damascus Document* clearly implies that the members of the 'camps' could possess money and goods, and could administer and increase them. But if the hypothesis which we have put forward is correct, and the 'camps' referred to in the Damascus Document represent the huts and tents set up along the rock cliffs, we should have discovered coins in the caves used by the inhabitants of these 'camps'. Should we then seek a different explanation for the absence of coins in the caves and suppose that at the moment of their flight the members of this special group hid their domestic wares and manuscripts but took their money with them? Is it possible that if we knew the site of these 'camps', now unfortunately indistinguishable, it would be here, and not in the caves (which served as store-places and hiding-places), that we should find the coins accidentally lost by them? If this were indeed the case, then the fact that coins are present in the buildings and never in the caves would lose all its force as an argument in support of the hypothesis that the people of Qumran were Essenes.

However, there is one particular case to which we must revert. It is the hoard of silver coins found in the building.[1] If it was brought there at the time of the reinstallation of Period II it may represent a capital sum collected by the community and not used by it. Alternatively it may have been deposited there at this time by a new adherent or adherents. In fact, according to the prescription laid down by the *Rule of the Community* the novice delivered his goods into the hands of the treasurer, but they were kept separate from the goods of the community, and were not spent until the novice had been definitively admitted. If this was the case in the present instance, the treasure hoard would, paradoxically, illustrate the practice of individual poverty.

[1] Cf. pp. 34–5.

The inscribed Copper Scroll found in Cave 3[1] is irrelevant to our present question. It makes no difference whether it derives from the community or had nothing to do with it, since the treasures listed in it, supposing them to be real, are certainly not the possessions of individuals.

We have seen that the community of Qumran relied in part for its sustenance on stock-rearing, certain types of cultivation, and certain industries. Josephus tells us that the Essenes practised agriculture. Philo tells us that they were agriculturalists, shepherds, and craftsmen. The evidence is consistent, but almost the entire population of Palestine followed the same occupations. Though the occupations at Qumran are the same as those described in our authorities, this does not establish that there was any religious connection between the people of Qumran and the Essenes.

Josephus also tells us that the Essenes took frequent baths for purposes of purification. The Qumran writings, both the *Damascus Document* and the *Rule of the Community*, speak of purifications by water. We have seen that there are a considerable number of cisterns at Khirbet Qumran, but the ordinary needs of any relatively numerous community living in a semi-desert region would be sufficient to explain the installation of a water system of this kind. One peculiar feature of the system has been emphasized by certain authors as an indication that they had a religious use. Apart from the round cistern, loc. 110, which is Israelite, and the large cistern to the south-west, loc. 91, which is a reservoir, all the cisterns (not counting the basins attached to them) are equipped with a large flight of steps descending into them and taking up at least half of their total length. Almost throughout, and perhaps actually so in their original state, the upper steps are divided by low partitions so as to form several parallel descents (Pl. xvi). These features have suggested that the cisterns were meant for ritual baths. However, we should not be too hasty in arriving at such a conclusion, for similar cisterns belonging to the same period are found especially in the neighbourhood of Jerusalem, having wide flights of steps leading down, and sometimes partitions on the steps,[2] and in these cases

---

[1] pp. 50–1, 108–9.
[2] Cf. the cistern at Bethany, *Revue biblique*, LVIII (1951), 200 ff., and the references supplied by R. P. Benoit in this connection, *ibid.* 204.

it cannot be said that they had any ritual function.[1] It is even doubtful whether they were intended for bathing in the secular sense.[2] More probably they were simple cisterns. The steps made it easier to draw water from them whatever the level of the water, and the partitions served to break and guide the flow while keeping one part of the steps dry. However, at Khirbet Qumran there are two smaller and more carefully designed basins with several flights of steps taking up almost their entire area (Pl. VIII). One of these is near the north-western entrance, loc. 138. The other is in the south-eastern quarter, loc. 68. They were certainly baths, but archaeology is powerless to determine whether the baths taken in them had a ritual significance.

Josephus records that at the beginning of their novitiate the Essene candidates received a hatchet, ἀξινάριον, a loin-cloth, and a white garment. This hatchet had a very special use. Josephus tells us that it was like a mattock, σκαλίς, and that the Essenes used to dig a hole in a desert spot each time they wished to relieve themselves. It was a literal application of the prescription in Deuteronomy 23: 13–14 relating to the purity of the camp. A further point is that, again according to Josephus, the Essenes were more rigorous than any other of the Jews in their observance of the sabbath, and 'dare not even move an object or go to stool', leaving us to understand that they held themselves back from this function on the sabbath day because they would have had to make use of their mattock. The term ἀξινάριον or ἀξινίδιον used by Josephus is a diminutive of the Greek ἀξίνη and the Latin *ascia*. It is a tool used in carpentry which can also be employed for digging or cutting roots, and which is known from archaeology and pictorial representations. The *Damascus Document* in its turn lays down strict rules for the observance of

---

[1] The most convincing case would be that of the two adjoining cisterns at the 'Tomb of Kings' at Jerusalem, which could have served for the purifications prescribed after burials, cf. E. Pfennigsdorff in *Zeitschrift des Deutschen Palästina-Vereins*, XXVII (1904), 184; M. Kon, *The Tomb of the Kings* (in Hebrew) (1947), 37. But Pfennigsdorff does not rule out a secular usage. The cisterns served a necessary function in drawing off the water which would otherwise have threatened to flood the monument, *loc. cit.*, 179.

[2] However, this is the explanation favoured by the excavators for the many cisterns of a similar type found at Samaria. Cf. J. W. Crowfoot, K. M. Kenyon, E. L. Sukenik, *The Buildings at Samaria* (1942), 134 and pl. lxxii. 2.

the sabbath, and in particular prohibits the carrying of any object if one leaves one's living quarters. In Cave 11 we discovered an iron tool identical in form with hatchets discovered in Roman territory and corresponding exactly to the instrument described by Josephus in connection with the Essenes.[1] Cave 11 was certainly occupied by the Qumran community, as is shown from the manuscripts and pottery found there,[2] but it cannot be proved that the hatchet which we found was a specifically Essene instrument. It could have been used by anyone in carpentry, the work for which it was primarily designed. But it is equally impossible to prove that it was not an Essene instrument. It conforms to Josephus' description of the ἀξινάριον, and could have served the same special use.

All this does not take us very far, and it is apparent that the same lack of certitude hangs over all the archaeological evidence which we might be tempted to invoke in order to establish that the Qumran community was Essene in character. There is nothing in the evidence to contradict such an hypothesis, but this is the only assured conclusion that we can arrive at on the basis of this evidence, and the only one which we can justifiably demand of it. The solution to the question is to be sought from the study of the texts, and not from that of the archaeological remains.

However, ruins generally still have a distinctive kind of evidence of their own to offer, and in the present case this is positive. In his *Natural History* Pliny the Elder describes the course of the Jordan and then of the Dead Sea and its eastern shore. He then goes on to describe the western shore:

Ab occidente litora Esseni fugiunt usque qua nocent, gens sola et in toto orbe praeter ceteras mira, sine ulla femina, omni venere abdicata, sine pecunia, socia palmarum. in diem ex aequo convenarum turba renascitur, large frequentantibus quos vita fessos ad mores eorum fortuna fluctibus agit. ita per saeculorum milia—incredibile dictu—gens aeterna est, in qua nemo nascitur. tam fecunda illis aliorum vitae paenitentia est! infra hos Engada oppidum fuit, secundum ab Hierosolymis fertilitate palmetorumque nemoribus, nunc alterum bustum.

[1] R. de Vaux, 'Une hachette essénienne?', *Vetus Testamentum*, IX (1959), 399–407.
[2] Cf. p. 51.

inde Masada castellum in rupe, et ipsum haud procul Asphaltite, et
hactenus Iudaea est.[1]

Pliny's information, therefore, is that the Essenes lived to the
west of the Dead Sea, some way back from the shore, in order
to protect themselves from the noxious effects of the water, of
which he has spoken. They live in isolation, having only the
palm trees for company. Lower down than their settlement
(*infra hos*) is the place known as En-Gedi. This can be taken, and
generally has been taken, as meaning that the Essene settlement
looked down upon En-Gedi which is in the littoral plain. In
other words it was located on higher ground to the west of
En-Gedi. Some go so far as to say that this is the only possible
interpretation. However, explorations and excavations recently
undertaken in the area of En-Gedi[2] have failed to reveal any
trace of an installation of any importance belonging to the
Roman period in the mountain overlooking the small tell known
as Tell el-Jurn from the west. Tell el-Jurn represents the
Israelite town of En-Gedi, and later, in the Roman period, the
capital of the district of Ἐνγαδδαί. Furthermore, Pliny states that
the Essenes lived in the company of the palm trees. There were
plenty of palm trees at En-Gedi, as Pliny says, and as had
already been said in one variant of Ben Sirach 24: 14. But these
palm trees were only able to grow on the lower ground round
the spring and the tell, which at that time was occupied. At no
time have there been any palm trees growing further to the west
on the rock cliffs. There is no site above En-Gedi which is both
isolated from human population and near to palm trees where
the Essenes could have lived.

The only course open to us, therefore, is to take the '*infra*' here
in the sense of 'to the south' or 'down stream'.[3] The phrase 'to

---

[1] *Hist. Nat.* v. xvii. 73, edited by Mayoff (Teubner).

[2] The explorations undertaken in ancient times have been summarized at
the beginning of the report on the recent excavations, B. Mazar, Tr. Dothan,
I. Dunayevsky, *En-Gedi. The First and Second Seasons of Excavations, 1961–1962*
= '*Atiqot*, English Series, v (1966). On the third season, cf. B. Mazar,
I. Dunayevsky, *Israel Exploration Journal*, XIV (1964), 121–30. In general,
B. Mazar, 'En-Gedi', *Archaeology and Old Testament Study*, ed. D. Winton
Thomas (1967), 223–30.

[3] This translation had been suggested by some interpreters long before the
discoveries at Qumran. In *Die Handschriften am Toten Meer* (1958), 39 n. 2,

the south of' is given, with references, in the *Thesaurus Linguae Latinae* as one of the senses of the preposition *infra*.[1] If this usage is contested, we still have the frequent use of the term *infra* in the sense of 'down stream of' in relation to a valley or a river. Now throughout this passage Pliny is describing the Jordan from its source down to the Dead Sea, into which it flows and which is connected with it. The two form a whole. On the west bank of this sea he first encounters the settlement of the Essenes, then, 'lower down than they', *infra hos*, En-Gedi, and then 'on leaving this', *inde*, Masada. And it is 'thus far', *hactenus*, that Judaea extends. Thus his description proceeds from north to south and presupposes that the Essenes were installed to the north-west of the Dead Sea and to the north of En-Gedi.[2]

Now between En-Gedi and the southernmost point of the Dead Sea there is only one site which corresponds to Pliny's description, and that is the plateau of Qumran, which is situated some way back from the shore and at a higher level, and which is healthier than the shore of the sea itself. I can bear personal witness to this, having myself camped first on the plateau of Qumran and then at Feshkha near the shore. Contrary to an interpretation which some have put forward, Pliny does not say that the Essenes are far from the shore. He says that they are just far enough away from it to ensure that they do not suffer from the exhalations of the sea, and this applies to the position of Khirbet Qumran. Furthermore, there is only one important group of buildings contemporary with Pliny between En-Gedi and the southernmost point of the Dead Sea, and that is the buildings of Khirbet Qumran and Feshkha.[3] There is only one

H. Bardtke quotes a German translation of Pliny published in 1853: 'Südlich von ihnen lag sonst die Stadt Engadda.'

[1] Vol. VII, i, fasc. x (1954), s.v. *infra*.

[2] The controversy on the sense of Pliny's text has been prolonged, apparently fruitlessly: J.-P. Audet, 'Qumrân et la notice de Pline sur les Esséniens', *Revue biblique*, LXVIII (1961), 346–87 (above En-Gedi); E.-M. Laperrousaz, '"Infra hos Engadda". Notes à propos d'un article récent', *ibid.*, LXIX (1962), 368–80 (Qumran); C. Burchardt, 'Pline et les Esséniens. A propos d'un article récent', *ibid.*, LXIX (1962), 533–69 (Qumran).

[3] In the appendix to chap. II (pp. 87–90) I have allowed for the possibility that the small buildings of Khirbet Mazin and 'Ain el-Ghuweir could have belonged to the same community as Qumran. In any case they would have been no more than annexes of very minor importance.

area where palm trees could grow in any quantity, and where we know that they were in fact cultivated in ancient times, and that is the area lying between Khirbet Qumran and Feshkha. If Pliny was not mistaken and if we are not mistaken, the Essenes of whom he speaks are the community of Qumran.

An objection has, however, been raised. A certain mutilated inscription has for a long time been the subject of discussion. In it Mommsen believed that he could recognize the name Pliny, and also an attestation of the fact that Pliny had fulfilled an important military function during the Jewish War on the staff of Titus.[1] The controversy has been reopened in the latest comprehensive study on Pliny,[2] in which the author concludes that Mommsen's hypothesis is very probably correct. On these grounds the objection has been raised that if Khirbet Qumran was destroyed in 68, if it was in fact the settlement of the Essenes, and if Pliny was in Judaea in 70, he would have mentioned this destruction, or at least he would not have spoken of the Essenes of the Dead Sea in the present tense and as though they were still a living community. His references to the settlement would have been the same as for En-Gedi, which he speaks of in the past tense, declaring that it is *nunc alterum bustum*. The term *alterum* here contains an implicit reference to Jerusalem, of which he is about to speak.[3] The ruin of Jerusalem is likewise presupposed in a passage close to the one we are considering.[4]

However, these allusions to the ruins of En-Gedi and Jerusalem respectively do not necessarily mean that Book v of the *Natural History*, together with this particular passage on the Essenes, were written after 70. This work of thirty-seven books has been re-edited over the course of many years. We know that Pliny himself was engaged in revising it down to the year 77, which is the date of his preface. But he did not revise all of it to

---

[1] E. Schürer, *Geschichte des jüdischen Volkes*, I⁵ (1920), 625, n. 87.

[2] W. Kroll, art. 'Plinius der Aeltere' in *Pauly-Wissowa*, XXI, i (1951), cols. 277–80.

[3] *secundum ab Hierosolymis fertilitate palmetorumque nemoribus, nunc alterum bustum.* Clearly it cannot be Jerusalem, but should rather be 'Jericho' that is credited with fertility and palm-groves. Yet the phrase '*nunc alterum bustum*' certainly refers to Jerusalem. The word 'Jerusalem', therefore, is not a scribal error. Rather it is a mistake on the part of Pliny himself or his source.

[4] *Hist. Nat.* v. xiv. 70: *in qua fuere Hierosolyma*, in the past tense.

the same extent. At this point he could have mentioned the fire at En-Gedi without altering the rest of his account in any way. And in fact immediately afterwards he speaks of Masada as a stronghold without recording the fact that it was destroyed in 73. In any case it makes little difference whether Pliny wrote this particular Book v, and this particular passage in it, before or after 70. It does not even make much difference whether or not he actually went to Judaea. If he did go there he did not see everything, and apart from informing us as to the place where the Essenes lived, his portrayal of them is an idealized one and does not show any signs of being an eye-witness account. There is no reason to believe that Pliny actually visited this Essene settlement. On the other hand he did not invent what he said about it. He is first and foremost a compiler. He repeats what he has read or heard. He is very credulous, and sometimes deficient in understanding, but he does not invent. He did not invent, and had no motive for inventing, the fact that the Essenes lived on the edge of the Dead Sea. And his reason for stating that this was so is that he has read it or heard it somewhere. If we suppose that his source of information was earlier than 68, and that it had not been revised, there is no difficulty in applying the passage in his work to the Qumran area.

Once more it must be recognized that this particular passage in Pliny is not *in itself* decisive. But if the writings of Qumran exhibit certain points of resemblance to what is known from other sources about the Essenes, and if the ruins of Qumran correspond to what Pliny tells us about the dwelling-place of the Essenes, his evidence can be accepted as true. And this evidence in its turn serves to confirm that the community was Essene in character. This is no vicious circle, but rather an argument by convergence, culminating in that kind of certitude with which the historian of ancient times often has to content himself.

There is no question of denying the differences which exist between the descriptions of the Essenes in Pliny, Philo, and Josephus on the one hand, and the portrait which can be reconstructed on the basis of the writings and ruins of Qumran on the other.[1] I believe that these differences can be explained by the

[1] Cf. especially M. H. Gottstein, 'Anti-Essene Traits in the Dead Sea Scrolls', *Vetus Testamentum*, IV (1954), 141–7; C. Roth, 'Were the Qumran

following factors: first that Essenism underwent an evolution, second that as a movement it contained within itself several different tendencies, and third that the evidence varies in quality. That of the classical authors comes from outside the movement and is more or less distorted. That of the Qumran writings has the community itself as its source. To demonstrate this would be to go beyond the purpose of this book, but at the conclusion of our study we are in a position to pose a question. This community, the life of which has been traced by archaeology over a period of some two centuries, and which has left behind a considerable literature, is no small unknown sect. It must belong to one of the movements which were important and well known within Judaism. Our judgement has been that the people of Qumran could not have been assimilated either to the Zealots, the Sadducees, or the Pharisees. If this is the case, what other movements are there with which they could have had connections except the Essenes who, according to Pliny's evidence, lived precisely in this area?

It is quite certain that in the study of the Qumran documents archaeology plays only a secondary role. But it has the advantage of supplying dates and bringing to bear certain material facts, the interpretation of which can be more objective than that of the texts, which are so often enigmatic or incomplete. It enables us to assure ourselves that the Qumran manuscripts are certainly authentic and that they are ancient, that they belonged to a religious community which lived beside the Dead Sea from the second half of the second century B.C. to A.D. 68, and that in all probability none of the manuscripts deposited in the caves is later than this date. The events in the life of the community, which took place at Qumran and are recounted in the manuscripts, must fall within this chronological framework. As to the possible doctrinal connections which this community may have had with other schools, all that archaeology can contribute is to provide a yardstick by which to test the conclusions arrived at from the documents. But inconclusive though it may be in this role, its evidence must still not be disregarded.

INDEX

(See also the Contents)

PLATES

PLATE I

Khirbet Qumran, general view looking east.

PLATE II

Khirbet Qumran at the end of the excavations. Aerial view.

PLATE III

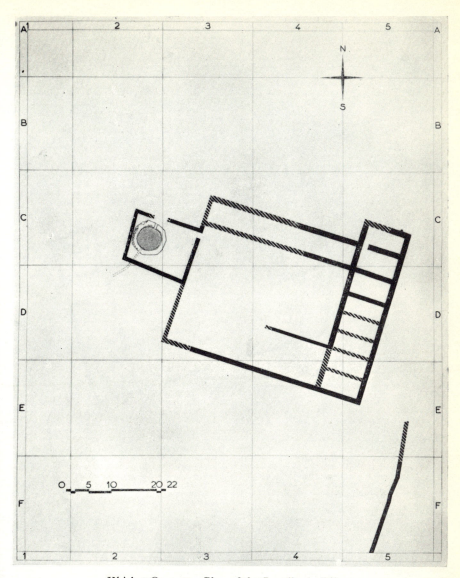

Khirbet Qumran. Plan of the Israelite building.

PLATE IV

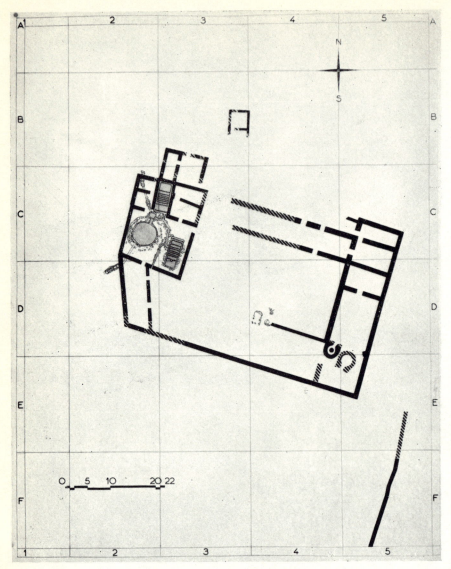

Khirbet Qumrân. Plan of Period I*a*.

PLATE V

a. Israelite cistern, loc. 110, with the decantation basin of Period I*a* in the foreground. View towards the south.

b. Potter's kiln from Period I*a*. Towards the south-west.

PLATE VI

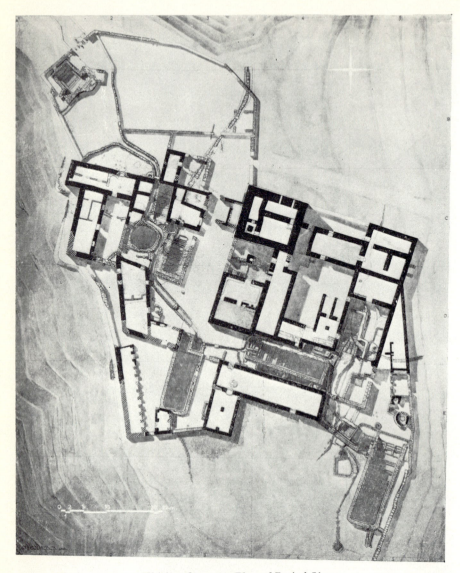

Khirbet Qumran. Plan of Period I*b*.

PLATE VII

a. The channel between cisterns 110 and 117. Towards the south-east.

b. The large cistern at 71. In the background the ruins. Towards the north-west.

PLATE VIII

a. Bath, loc. 138. Towards the south-west.

b. Bath, loc. 68. Towards the east.

PLATE IX

a. Assembly room, loc. 77. Towards the east.

b. Annexe to the assembly room, locs. 86 and 89. Towards the south.

PLATE X

a. Broken bowls in the south-eastern corner of loc. 89.

b. Piles of dishes against the southern wall of loc. 89.

PLATE XI

a. Deposits of animal bones in loc. 130. Towards the west. In the foreground, debris from the clearing out of the building at the beginning of Period II.

b. A deposit of animal bones with sherds laid over them.

PLATE XII

General view of the potter's workshop. Towards the south-west.

PLATE XIII

a. Basin for levigating clay, loc. 75. Towards the south-east.

b. The site of the potter's wheel in loc. 65. Towards the south.

PLATE XIV

a. The large potter's kiln, loc. 64. View from above and towards the north-west.

b. The small potter's kiln, loc. 84. Towards the north.

PLATE XV

a. Tableware from Period I*b*, coming from the store of crockery found in loc. 89.

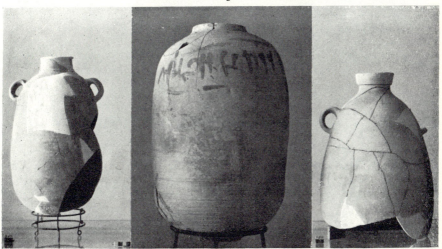

b. Large jars from Period I*b*.

PLATE XVI

Cistern 48–49, split by the earthquake. Towards the south-west.

PLATE XVII

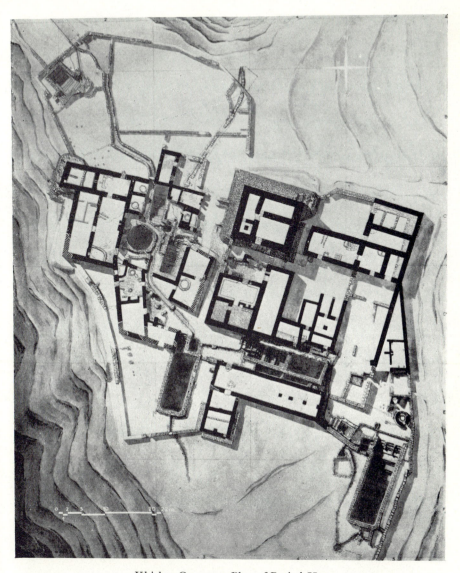

Khirbet Qumran. Plan of Period II.

PLATE XVIII

Khirbet Qumran. Cisterns and workshops between the buildings. Towards the south-west.

PLATE XIX

a. Workshop in loc. 101. Towards the south.

b. Workshop in loc. 125. Towards the north.

PLATE XX

a. Base of the mill, loc. 100. Towards the north-west.

b. Basalt millstone thrown down in loc. 104.

PLATE XXI

a. Writing tables and bench from loc. 30.

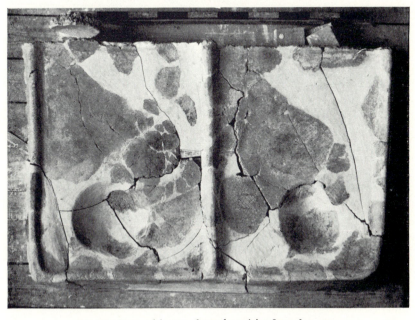

b. Platform with cup-shaped cavities from loc. 30.

PLATE XXII

a. Pottery from Period II.

b. On the right, a jar from Period II with the square piece of
limestone used to close it. On the left, a jar with a flat lid from
Cave I.

PLATE XXIII

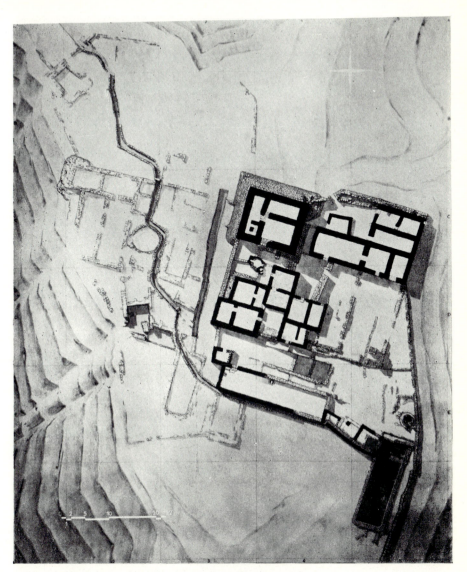

Khirbet Qumran. Plan of Period III.

PLATE XXIV

a. Debris thrown out by the Romans and found in the north-western corner of cistern 58.

b. The beginning of the Roman conduit in loc. 100.

PLATE XXV

a. Tomb in the main cemetery before the excavation. Towards the south-east.

b. Tomb 29 opened up: the loculus covered with stones. Towards the east.

PLATE XXVI

a. Tomb 27 opened up: the loculus covered with mud bricks. Towards the east.

b. Tomb 21 after clearing: the skeleton. Towards the east.

PLATE XXVII

a. The position of Cave 1. The entrance is low down and to the left. Towards the north-east.

b. The entrance of Cave 11. Towards the north.

PLATE XXVIII

Caves in the marl terrace: Cave 4 in the centre, at the point where the figure is standing; Cave 5 in the isolated massif on the extreme right. To the left, Wadi Qumrân. Towards the west.

PLATE XXIX

a. Smaller pieces of pottery from the caves.

b. Jar and lids from the caves.

PLATE XXX

a. The long wall running away from Wadi Qumran towards the south.

b. The square building. Towards the south-east.

PLATE XXXI

The area between 'Ain Feshkha and Khirbet Qumran (upper left). Towards the north.

PLATE XXXII

a. Feshkha. General view of the excavations. Towards the north-east.

b. The building at Feshkha. Towards the north-west.

PLATE XXXIII

a. Feshkha: the northern half of the building.   Towards the west.

b. Locs. 21–22.   Towards the east.

PLATE XXXIV

a. Stone vase from Feshkha.

b. Pottery from Feshkha. Below, centre, a Byzantine gourd.

PLATE XXXV

a. Feshkha, loc. 15 (Period III). Towards the south-east.

b. Roman weight.   *c.* Hoard of coins of Agrippa II.

PLATE XXXVI

a. Feshkha: the shed on the south. Towards the west. In the foreground the room which was reoccupied in the Byzantine period, loc. 20.

b. The eastern part of the shed. Towards the north-east.

PLATE XXXVII

a. Feshkha: basins and channels of the northern enclosure. Towards the east. In the foreground, the inlet for the water, loc. 29. Cf. Pl. XXXVIII*b.*

b. The same basins and channels towards the west. In the centre, the large cylindrical stones.

PLATE XXXVIII

a. Basins 24, 25, 27. Towards the west.

b. The inlet for the water, loc. 29. Towards the south.